D0044678

**THE BRITISH LIBRARY**
**HISTORIC LIVES**

# Sir Francis Drake

THE BRITISH LIBRARY
HISTORIC LIVES

# Sir Francis Drake

**Peter Whitfield**

Cover illustration: Portrait of Drake.
Artist unknown, c. 1580.
*National Portrait Gallery*

Endpaper illustration: Francis
Fletcher's narrative of the first part
of Drake's second voyage round the
world, exactly copied from the
original by John Conyers, citizen
and apothecary of London, 1677.
*The British Library, Sloane MS 61,
ff.38v–39*

Half-title page illustration:
The Hondius portrait, undated but
showing Drake aged forty-two.
*British Museum*

Title-page illustration:
The painting attributed to Nicholas
Hilliard of the defeat of the Armada,
watched from the shore by Queen
Elizabeth.
*Society of Apothecaries/
bridgeman.co.uk*

First published in 2004 by
The British Library
96 Euston Road
London NW1 2DB

Designed and typeset
by Andrew Barron @ thextension

Printed in Hong Kong
by South Sea International Press

First published in the U.S.A.
in 2004 by
NEW YORK UNIVERSITY PRESS
Washington Square, New York
www.nyupress.org

Text © Peter Whitfield 2004
Illustrations © The British Library
Board and other named copyright
holders 2004

Library of Congress Cataloging-in-
Publication Data
Whitfield, Peter, Dr.
Sir Francis Drake/Peter Whitfield.
p. cm. – (Historic lives)
Includes bibliographical references
(p. ) and index.
ISBN 0-8147-9403-3 (alk. paper)
1. Drake, Francis, Sir, 1540?–1596.
2. Great Britain–History,
Naval–Tudors, 1485-1603–
Biography. 3. Elizabeth I, Queen of
England, 1533–1603–Relations
with explorers. 4. Great Britain–
History–Elizabeth, 1558–1603–
Biography. 5. Privateering–History
–16th century. 6. Explorers–Great
Britain–Biography. 7. Admirals–
Great Britain–Biography. I. Title.
II. Series.
DA86.22.D7W47 2004
942.05'5'092–dc22  2004049930
[B]

# Contents

**1** The young adventurer (*c.*1540–77)  6

**2** To the fearful strait (1577–78)  38

**3** An Englishman in the Pacific (1578–85)  62

**4** Open warfare (1585–87)  90

**5** The Armada campaign (1587–88)  112

**6** Last voyages and the Drake legend (1588–96)  128

*Chronology*  156

*Further reading*  157

*Index*  158

... a man of action, a conqueror, and a celebrity, but also something of an enigma, and a man with unmistakable flaws.

# The young adventurer
# c. 1540—77

*His name was a terror to the French, Spaniard, Portugal and Indians. Many princes of Italy, Germany and others, as well enemies as friends, desired his picture. He was the second that ever went through the Straits of Magellan ... In brief, he was famous in Europe and America as Tamburlaine in Asia and Africa. In his imperfections, he was ambitious for honour, unconstant in amity, and greatly affected to popularity.*

This was the impressive but decidedly ambiguous portrait of Sir Francis Drake penned just a few years after his death by the Elizabethan historian, Edmund Howes. It suggests that Drake was not only a man of action, a conqueror, and a celebrity, but also something of an enigma, and a man with unmistakable flaws. Four centuries later the enigma of Francis Drake remains unresolved. His career as a maritime explorer and military leader elevated him long ago to the status of an English national hero, one of the stars in the brilliant constellation of the Elizabethan age. Drake's final apotheosis came in the nineteenth century, when historians and popularisers alike chose to portray him as nothing less than the founder of the Royal Navy and of the British Empire. The celebrations in 1888 and again in 1988, marking the anniversaries of the Spanish Armada, served to reinforce this image of Drake in the public mind.

In the last twenty years, however, critical scholarship has raised deep suspicions of this legend. In place of the fearless explorer, innovative naval strategist and pioneer of empire, we have now been offered the portrait of a man who was undoubtedly tenacious, full of energy and audacity, but who was really little more than a pirate, an aggressive intimidator, whose rapacious career was glorified by his countrymen because of the historical circumstances in which it was played out. It has to be said that this revolution in our view of Drake has not come about through the discovery of any dramatic new evidence. Most of Drake's voyages and exploits are extremely well documented, and many of these

Previous page: Portrait of Drake by
Nicholas Hilliard, 1581. The famous
miniaturist was a Devon man like Drake,
and they may have been good friends.
Hilliard named his son, born in 1580,
Francis. Hilliard's Drake looks like a
slim, refined courtier.
*National Portrait Gallery*

documents have been in the public domain for centuries. Rather, it has come
about through a hard look at the historical context in which Drake cut his way
to fame, through a cool reassessment of his motives, and through a revaluation of
our ideas of heroism and nationalism: in the twenty-first century, many of Drake's
great deeds look little better than acts of mercenary or guerrilla warfare. Moreover,
these modern criticisms are personal as well as political, for no study of Drake
can avoid focusing on certain crucial, mysterious episodes in Drake's life which
have never been explained, and where he seems to have been guilty of cowardice,
paranoia, greed or dishonesty. One of the problems with Drake is that we have
virtually no words of his own or documents from his own hand. The man's
personality, his inner life, his ideas and motives, are hidden from us: all we have
are his actions, and their interpretation is open to deep disagreement.

What then is the correct approach to Drake today? Is the fashionable, coldly
critical view really more valid than the old-fashioned hero-worship? There is no
shortage of source material, for the construction of the Drake legend began early,
and we have a semi-official account of his career in a number of contemporary
texts, such as *The World Encompassed*, the narrative of the great circumnavigation,
which still form the basis for all later studies. These works offered a lively
account of Drake's principal adventures, and they assured his high place both
in official historiography and in popular fame. Contemporary historians such as
William Camden and John Stow also had a good deal to say about Drake, but
their stories are sometimes implausible and usually unverifiable. Thus, while
there is no dispute about the broad outline of his career, a nest of problems
and obscurities stubbornly refuse to be solved, especially those concerning
his aims and motives, and his ultimate significance. It is this uncertainty which
has given rise to so many versions of Drake's character and importance, from

the hero-worship of the Victorian historians to the cold iconoclasm of today.

The central fact to grasp about Drake is that he was a man of action, not a man of ideas; yet those actions reverberated across Europe and down the centuries. Drake's life shows that energy, ambition and fierce self-interest can sway the course of history, even where these are not directed by high motives or grand strategy. It also shows how powerfully symbols can act on a nation's consciousness. In Drake's career, the man and the moment met, and he profoundly influenced England's role in world history by inspiring his countrymen with the belief that their destiny was entwined with the sea. The time may well have come to cast a cold eye on heroes and hero-worship, but that surely gives us the opportunity to arrive at a clear-sighted judgement on this enigmatic figure.

The first of the puzzles surrounding Francis Drake concerns his youth and upbringing. The Elizabethan historian, William Camden, summed up the account which became universally accepted:

*This Drake (to relate no more than what I have learned from himself) was born of mean parentage in Devonshire ... while he was yet a child, his father, imbracing the Protestant doctrine, fled his country and withdrew himself into Kent ... he got a place among the sailors in the king's fleet, to read prayers unto them, and soon after was ordained deacon, and made vicar of the church of Upnore upon the River Medway (where the fleet lyeth at anchor).*

Camden claimed that these facts were given to him by Drake himself, while other similar stories, from the chronicler John Stow for example, relate how Francis's father, Edmund Drake, lived for some years with his family in the hulk of an abandoned ship in the Medway; that he had fled Devon in 1549 during

Previous page: Plymouth and the
surrounding countryside at the time of
Drake's birth; part of the survey of
Britain's southern coasts commissioned
in the 1540s by King Henry VIII.
*The British Library, Cotton MS Aug.1.i.35*

violent reactions by Catholics against the new Protestant religion; that Francis
Drake was apprenticed to a mariner plying the Thames estuary and the east coast,
who, having no sons of his own, bequeathed his ship to his hard-working young
companion. However, none of these stories is supported by any independent
evidence. Camden's 'Upnore' is a mistake for Upchurch, a village south of the
Medway estuary, where Edmund Drake became vicar in 1560. Drake's family
was of farming stock, from Crowndale near Tavistock, in Devon, where Edmund
Drake was described in contemporary records as a shearsman, and it is extremely
difficult to understand how such a man could have become an ordained priest
of the Anglican church, a profession normally reserved for men of university
education. Camden's story is doubly puzzling given the notorious persecution
of Protestants during the reign of Queen Mary from 1553 to 1558: how could
Edmund Drake have made a living prayer-reading and acting as a Protestant
pastor to sailors of the royal fleet, in a town so close to London, without being
denounced? The picture has been made still more confused by the recent
discovery that a certain Edmund Drake, shearsman, was indicted for two separate
highway robberies near Tavistock, during which Drake and some companions
threatened and beat their victims, and made off with cash in one case and a horse
in the other. These events occurred in April 1548, and immediately afterwards,
Edmund Drake fled the county.

It is impossible to say whether this Edmund Drake was Francis Drake's
father, or to confirm his occupation as a farmer, a highway robber or a priest, or
to know whether he was all three in succession. If he left Devon to escape justice
in 1548, then he would clearly not have been affected by the pro-Catholic
disturbances there, which took place in 1549. It is possible that the story of his
flight from religious persecution was a mere invention, designed to cover a much

The plain fact is that Francis Drake was, as Camden stated, 'of mean parentage', and therefore the surviving records of his childhood and youth are inevitably as scant and obscure as those of any other commoner born four and a half centuries ago.

more sordid past. We do know that when Edmund Drake, vicar of Upchurch, died in 1566, his will made no mention whatever of a son named Francis, but left the execution of his wishes in the hands of his son Thomas. The name of Drake's mother is unknown, although some slight circumstantial evidence suggests that she may have been Anna Millway, also of a Devon farming family. Even the date of Francis Drake's birth is uncertain, because the many contemporary sources which give a date disagree with each other, and around 1540 is as near as we can get.

From a very early date, all the Drake records make great play of the fact that Francis and his relatives were kinsmen of the Hawkins family, the dynasty of Plymouth seafarers whose activities were to play such an important role in Francis's early career, yet the exact degree of the relationship has never been established. The name of the east-coast seafarer who supposedly bequeathed Drake his ship was not recorded, nor any of the places where Drake sailed as a youth. The date and the circumstances in which he left Kent and returned to Plymouth are unknown, and there is even some slight evidence that he may not have accompanied his father to Kent at all, but remained in Plymouth to be brought up within the Hawkins household.

The plain fact is that Francis Drake was, as Camden stated, 'of mean parentage', and therefore the surviving records of his childhood and youth are inevitably as scant and obscure as those of any other commoner born four and a half centuries ago. Around the early life of any such figure who later achieves fame, certain legends will grow, perhaps encouraged by the man himself, making it now virtually impossible to distinguish fact from fiction. We know that the mature Drake was a great sailor and an ardent Protestant, and he must have learned his seafaring and his religion from somewhere, but, unfortunately, the historical record does not give us any clear answers as to where. Francis Drake

Phillip II, King of Spain from 1556–98.
His immense power and his Catholic
zeal overshadowed European history
and formed the essential backdrop to
Drake's career.
*British Museum*

finally steps out of the mists of
uncertainty into history around the
year 1560, as a young man of about
twenty, sailing out of Plymouth with his
'kinsman', John Hawkins, on voyages to
the Canary Islands and the West African
coast. By exploring the context of these
voyages, and the nature of the maritime
world which Drake chose to enter in
these early years of Queen Elizabeth's
reign, it is possible to gain a better
understanding of Drake's character.

Half a century before Drake's
birth, world geopolitics had been
revolutionised by the epoch-making
voyages of discovery undertaken by
the Portuguese and the Spanish. The former had found the Indian Ocean route
to the Spice Islands, while the latter had carved out an overseas empire in the
Americas. Both these geographical realms were claimed as monopolies, a claim
enforced by Papal authority and respected among the Catholic kings of Europe.
This situation was transformed by the Reformation, and by the tremendous
enmity which it created between the Catholic and Protestant nations. It was
William Cecil, Lord Burghley, Queen Elizabeth's leading statesman, who told
the Spanish ambassador that 'the Pope had no authority to divide up the world'.
The conflict between England and Spain provides the inescapable backdrop to
England's maritime history in the later sixteenth century, and to the career of

Francis Drake. Spain was the temporal champion of the Catholic Church, and the historical accident of Spanish rule in the Netherlands made her threat to England all the more dangerous. The growth of Protestantism in the Netherlands forged a natural alliance between her and England. This conflict issued into open warfare only briefly in the year of the Armada, but for decades it was channelled into guerrilla war waged against Spain's overseas interests. The enormous wealth which flowed into Spain's treasury from the Americas became a great object of English envy – 'the golden harvest which they get out of the earth and send into Spain to trouble all the earth', as one contemporary expressed it. The shadow of Spain, immeasurably deepened by the events of Mary Tudor's reign, was omnipresent in the English mind, and justification for the long catalogue of acts of plunder, piracy and covert warfare was claimed on the grounds that the victim was a political and religious enemy. In Drake, resentment of Spain became a passion, whether it was inherited from a fiercely Protestant father or not, and we know that John Foxe's graphic history of the Marian martyrs (Protestants martyred during the reign of Queen Mary) was Drake's constant companion at home and aboard ship.

The greatest of all of acts of plunder in the sixteenth century had occurred within England itself: the seizure of religious property by Queen Elizabeth's father King Henry VIII. This act revolutionised much of the economic and social life of the nation, and its psychological effect was enormous, as here, endorsed by royal example, was the clearest possible proof that plunder, and in the guise of religious zeal, could become a career, a path to wealth and power; the lesson was surely not lost on Drake. It was King Henry too who reorganised the navy, making the Admiralty a department of state, building new dockyards and sponsoring naval architects to improve ship design. Henry greatly extended the system of authorising private vessels to trade or make war in the national interest and this naval culture of privateering exactly mirrored the practice of raising ad hoc armies commanded by friends of the Crown to fight on land. Privateering reflected the amorphous nature of the Tudor state – the dispersal of power through the members of an aggressive ruling class, who were satellites of the monarch. Throughout Drake's career, the question of his official or unofficial status was never finally settled: it became a kind of diplomatic game, played between Queen Elizabeth and the Spanish authorities. Undoubtedly she sponsored and rewarded Drake privately, but when the Spanish protested about his acts of plunder, she could truthfully deny that he held any official position.

It was against this background that England transformed itself during the years 1540 to 1600 into an ocean-going world power, and in this process Drake's example was central. When this period began, the English were far less conscious of the revolution in navigation, and in the sciences generally, than their European neighbours, and in 1540 English sailors rarely ventured beyond the coasts of western Europe. By 1600 practitioners of the pure and the applied sciences in England had caught up, and English mariners were exploring and trading to the Baltic and to Russia, in the Mediterranean and West Africa, in the Caribbean and on the Atlantic coast of North America, and in the Indian Ocean, as well as valiantly pursuing the vain attempt to find northern sea routes to the Pacific via Canada and Russia. Statesmen, courtiers and intellectuals became deeply interested in exploration, seeing it as a vital tool of national power, a belief epitomised with the publication in 1589 of Richard Hakluyt's great work *The Principal Navigations Voyages and Discoveries of the English Nation*, in which Hakluyt argued that it was England's special destiny to explore and colonise North America.

English seamen had long cultivated traditional piloting knowledge, which was adequate for sailing in European coastal waters, but ocean voyages out of sight of land for weeks demanded very different navigational skills for determining latitude and longitude. Belatedly, English seafarers began to learn the science of ocean navigation from their Iberian counterparts, from the books by Martin Cortes and Pedro da Medina, which were translated into English in the 1560s and 1570s. Even later, a supposedly original English work like John Davis's influential book, *The Seaman's Secrets*, 1595, was largely a translation of Medina's fundamental work on navigation. The military importance and the economic importance of the sea went hand in hand. 'He that commands the sea is at great liberty,' wrote Francis Bacon, 'and may take as much and as little of the war as he will; whereas those that be strongest by land are many times nevertheless in great straits.' From the sixteenth century onwards, European powers conducted their wars overseas, preying on each other's colonies, trade routes and sources of wealth. This was the great lesson which Drake had to teach, and which transformed England into a nation for whom the sea was central to her life. The vital role of the sea in England's national strategy was expressed most succinctly two centuries later by Napoleon: 'It is necessary for us to be masters of the sea for six hours only, and England will have ceased to exist.'

Much of the initial impetus in the Elizabethan English seafaring revolution came from the ports in the west of England, from Bristol and Plymouth in particular. It seems that London merchants were at first wary of antagonising Spain by overseas adventures, for fear of endangering their rich wool trade with the Spanish-controlled Netherlands. The west-country seafarers had no such inhibitions, and shipowners such as the Hawkins family set out in search of exotic cargoes wherever they might find them, even in Spanish or Portuguese spheres of power. It was in a series of such voyages between 1560 and 1568 that Drake

Queen Elizabeth I, resting her hand
confidently upon the globe. England's
rise to international power would owe a
great deal to Drake. This is one of the
many triumphant images of the queen
painted after the Armada, seen here in
the background.
*bridgeman.co.uk*

The *Jesus of Lubeck*, the royal ship of 700 tons which Hawkins captained in his early voyages to West Africa and the Caribbean. It was abandoned in the fateful action at San Juan de Ulua. *Magdalene College, Cambridge*

gained his first and formative experience of seafaring beyond Europe, of the world of ocean navigation, trade negotiations, piracy, slaving, and armed conflict with local rulers and with all-powerful Spain. It was a cut-throat world of high potential rewards and high potential danger, in which the gentlemen and the rogues risked their lives in the scramble for fortune.

Anecdotal evidence from the Elizabethan chroniclers Howes and Camden tells us that Drake served as a seaman on these voyages in Hawkins's ships. The Englishmen carried mainly cloth, but also manufactured goods such as knives and tools, and trinkets with which to trade. The Canaries or the Azores, despite official Portuguese and Spanish disapproval, were excellent international markets, but there is no doubt that piracy was as great a lure as honest trade, and that any Spanish or French merchant vessel encountered by Hawkins and his men in their well-armed ships was almost certain to be attacked and robbed. From the Atlantic islands, it was a short step to trade on the African coast itself, and John Hawkins was not the only Englishman to visit the Guinea coast and bring home valuable cargoes of ivory, gold and pepper.

Officially this West African trade was, once again, a Portuguese monopoly, but merchants everywhere would buy and sell if the price was right, turning a blind eye to the regulations. John Hawkins knew this, and it inspired his master plan: to break into the African slave trade. In 1562 he enlisted the aid of highly placed figures in London to finance an ambitious voyage in which he would furnish several large ships, while his contacts in the Canaries would provide supplies and skilled navigators with knowledge of the local sea routes to transport slaves from West Africa to the Caribbean, where they would be sold at favourable prices to Spanish settlers in the islands and on the mainland. Among the men known to have been involved in the planning of this expedition were Hawkins's own father-in-law, Benjamin Gonson, and William Wynter, respectively the treasurer and the surveyor of the English navy.

Hawkins's fleet of four ships left Plymouth in October 1562, and his plan was carried out with great overall success. Slaves were either captured by the English, or were stolen from Portuguese vessels, and they were sold at ports in Hispaniola at below the market price to the willing Spanish buyers. Hawkins returned to Plymouth in September 1563 a rich man, and wasted no time in preparing for a second, larger voyage. Such had been his earlier success that this

Such had been his (Hawkins) earlier
success that this time one of his
sponsors was none other than Queen
Elizabeth herself, who lent the 700-
ton royal ship, the Jesus of Lubeck ...

time one of his sponsors was none other than Queen Elizabeth herself, who lent the 700-ton royal ship, the *Jesus of Lubeck* (so named because it had been purchased from the league of Hansa merchants). This second voyage was essentially a rerun of the first, and gave Hawkins and his backers a good return on their investment. But by this time the Spanish and Portuguese had become seriously concerned at this English invasion of their overseas trade, and their London ambassadors made their displeasure known to the queen. Throughout her reign, Queen Elizabeth, although most willing to wound Spain, was very reluctant to strike openly, and so risk full-scale war. In this case therefore, Hawkins was diplomatically reprimanded, and a promise was extracted from him not to revisit the Caribbean that year. He complied, then covertly furnished another man, John Lovell (reportedly another of his 'kinsmen') with a small fleet to undertake a third expedition for him.

Drake's presence on the earlier voyages has been generally assumed, but from this Lovell voyage there exists firm, independent testimony that the young Drake was indeed on board one of the ships. Reports of this expedition are rather confused, but it was clearly less successful than the previous ones: at various ports on the Venezuelan coast and on Hispaniola, Lovell had to resort to armed force to compel the Spanish to trade with him. When he arrived back in Plymouth in the summer of 1567, Hawkins was disappointed with the results and immediately began preparations for a fresh attempt to break into the Caribbean slave trade, which he himself would lead. This voyage was to develop in a very different way from the earlier ones, culminating in a sequence of violent events that would prove to be a turning point in Drake's life, as in Hawkins's.

The fleet consisted of six ships: the *Jesus of Lubeck* was Hawkins's flagship; the *Minion* was a second royal vessel; four of Hawkins's own ships made up the

Map of the Caribbean showing the
principal places associated with Drake.
*Map drawn by Cedric Knight*

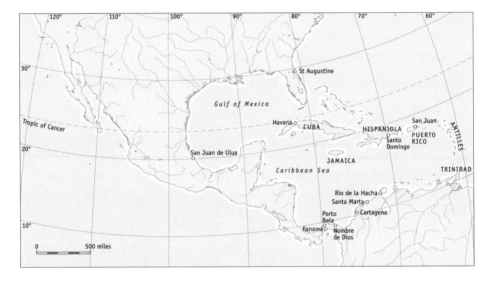

remainder, including the *Judith*, which was reportedly captained by Drake himself. The voyage began badly, and it grew progressively worse. Only four days out of Plymouth, the fleet was damaged and separated by severe storms, and when they regrouped in Tenerife, Hawkins found the Spanish extremely hostile and was only able to take on fresh supplies with difficulty. Sailing on to the Guinea coast, a raiding party to capture slaves met with fierce resistance, and several of Hawkins's men were killed or wounded. Enough captives were at last secured to turn and set a course across the Atlantic.

Hawkins in his stateroom lived in some luxury, with wines, fine linen and silver on his table, and musicians to play for him. Protestant religion was an important feature of life aboard the ships, and each day saw an hour's prayer-reading and psalm-singing among the crew. It is a bizarre picture: the epicurean slave trader quaffing his wines, and joining his pious crew for prayers, while below decks, hundreds of miserable prisoners lay crammed in darkness and filth, as they were carried to their life of slavery.

Arriving on the Venezuelan coast in April 1568, Hawkins was faced with the same hostility that Lovell had encountered. Diplomacy and threats were used to persuade the Spanish colonists to buy, but without success. Finally, at the port of Rio de la Hacha, Hawkins lost patience, landed several hundred armed men and stormed the town, burning buildings and taking hostages. Under this compulsion, the Spanish agreed to buy slaves and other goods if Hawkins would only depart, and this pattern was repeated at Santa Marta and Cartagena until Hawkins decided that his coffers were full enough to turn for home. Planning to sail north of Cuba and through the Straits of Florida, the fleet had barely passed the Yucatan Channel when it was overtaken by a fierce hurricane. One of the ships became totally separated, and made a lonely voyage home, while several of the others, including the *Jesus of Lubeck*, were so badly damaged that Hawkins felt compelled to find a port in which to make repairs. His choice of a port was a fateful one: turning south he made for San Juan de Ulua, the port of Vera Cruz, effectively the maritime capital of Spanish Mexico.

Although structurally damaged, Hawkins's ships were well armed, and he was able, on 17 September, to take possession of the small island which lay opposite the port. Here he planned to refit and resupply for the homeward voyage, but the whole situation was transformed the very next day by the arrival of a fleet from Spain, bearing the newly appointed viceroy of New Spain himself, Martin Enriquez. Messages passed between the two fleets, and Enriquez agreed to allow the English to carry out their planned repairs on the island, while his own ships proceeded into harbour proper. As a guarantee of peace, hostages were exchanged, but the English were alarmed and deeply suspicious – and with reason – for they guessed correctly that Enriquez would not wish to commence his governorship by cooperating with a fleet of foreign pirates. On the morning of 23 September, the Spanish attacked the island with cannon and with foot soldiers. Some of the English retreated desperately into their ships, and attempted escape. The flagship, the *Jesus of Lubeck*, was set ablaze by a Spanish fireship, and Hawkins escaped to the *Minion* with as much of the treasure from the voyage as he could carry. Others escaped to Drake's ship, the *Judith*, which was nearby. Taken by surprise, ill-prepared and outnumbered, the English position was hopeless, and all who could scrambled aboard the *Minion* or the *Judith*, as they struggled clear of the battle. Hundreds of men were left behind, as were four English ships, captured or destroyed by the Spanish.

What happened in the immediate aftermath of the battle was never fully explained, and it is one of the crucial puzzles of Drake's career: sometime in the evening or later that night, the *Judith* sailed away from the *Minion*, and disappeared into the darkness. Hawkins's ship, battle-damaged, leaking, desperately overcrowded and lacking in food and water, drifted slowly out into the Gulf of Mexico alone, her chances of making the voyage home virtually nil. About half of the men asked to be put ashore on the north-east coast of Mexico and take their chances there, rather than risk the Atlantic, and Hawkins agreed. This decision probably saved him and his ship, for almost four months later the *Minion* limped into Mounts Bay, Cornwall, after a nightmare voyage which would normally have taken four weeks. 'The *Judith*,' Hawkins later wrote, 'forsook us in our great miserie'. Drake himself never explained his actions. Was it cowardice and a plain case of desertion? Could he have helped the *Minion* anyway? How did the *Judith* navigate her way safely back to Plymouth? Did Drake manage to reap any substantial rewards from the voyage? All these questions remained unanswered, and the affair would come back to haunt Drake throughout his life. His friendship with Hawkins was ended, and Hawkins himself never returned to the Caribbean again for almost thirty years, and when he did so, it claimed his life. But Drake and Hawkins were at least alive and in England: for several hundred English sailors, the battle was only the beginning of a longer nightmare. Some starved in the forests or were killed by Indians, while those who were captured were sent back to Spain to face torture, perpetual imprisonment or the flames of the Inquisition. To his credit, Hawkins made prolonged diplomatic efforts to secure the release of some of these men.

Drake always spoke with deep bitterness about the duplicity of the Spanish at San Juan de Ulua, and he would spend years seeking private revenge for what happened. But perhaps he also had something to expiate – an act of treachery towards his oldest friend and mentor. Whatever the truth about this episode, there is no doubt that it turned Drake's ambitions into a new channel. Thereafter, Spain and all things Spanish became his prey; slaving and trading voyages no longer interested him, and he would dedicate himself to attacking and plundering Spanish possessions in whatever corner of the world he found them. An ignoble ambition perhaps, but the circumstances of European politics in the 1570s and 1580s, combined with Drake's personal brilliance and tenacious character, served to transform it into a plan of historic importance.

The official sequel to the events at San Juan de Ulua are unclear. Hawkins and Drake petitioned the government for redress for their financial losses, which Hawkins claimed amounted to £25,000. Their hope was that the queen would either raise the matter officially with Spain, or issue a 'commission of reprisal' – effectively a licence for the English sailors to attack and seize goods from any

Oceanì incogni

Terra de florid

Noua galiti

Nouagaliti

Sinus magnus ãtiliarũ

TROPICVS CANCII

Mericop. s

Nouabispan

Occanus occidẽtis

Mare de sul

LINIA EQVINOCIALIS

Mare austrum

Magnū mare occidẽtale

TROPICVS CAPRICORNI

ORIENS

Mare. m. meridioms.

Navigatio de magalhoẽs.

MERIDIES

OCCIDENS

Spanish ships they could find. But their wish was not granted. England was effectively at peace with Spain, and the fact that such a battle could take place without provoking outright war underlines the strangely unofficial nature of events that took place overseas, and how they failed to determine policy in Europe itself. Hawkins turned his knowledge to naval administration, and achieved a powerful position as treasurer of the navy, designing and supplying ships.

Many reports began to circulate that Hawkins and Drake had after all managed to bring home a substantial treasure and, undoubtedly, Drake now took certain steps which suggests that he was not destitute. First, on 4 July 1569 at St Budeaux Church in Plymouth, he married. Virtually nothing is known about his bride, Mary Newman, except that her family seems to have been established in the Plymouth area. (No children were born of this, or of Drake's second marriage.) His second step, only a few months after his wedding, was to fit out an expedition to return to the Caribbean. As Drake's semi-official biographer, Philip Nichols, put it: 'Finding that no recompense could be recovered out of Spain, he used such helps as he might, by two several voyages into the West Indies, to gain such intelligences as might further him to get some amends for his loss.'

There were probably two such voyages between 1569 and 1571. They are ill-documented, but they must have given Drake extremely valuable knowledge about the geography and administration of New Spain. He learned the size and strength of many of the ports, and how easy or difficult it might be to attack Spanish ships anchored there. He learned that this extensive coastline was in fact virtually unpatrolled and undefended by the Spanish, who still felt quite secure in their maritime monopoly, so that a single well-armed English ship had an excellent chance of attacking ports and shipping, and then escaping. He learned that there existed innumerable small bays and coves where such a raiding ship might hide and rest her crew. He learned that in the jungles of New Spain there lived many thousands of escaped slaves, called *cimarrones*, thirsty for revenge on their former masters, and who were therefore great potential allies. But the central fact upon which Drake fastened was the vital strategic importance of the Isthmus of Panama, the narrowest neck of land in the entire American continent, where just thirty miles of forest separated the Atlantic and the Pacific Oceans. This mere thread of land was a key part in the Spanish imperial system, for through it was transported the gold and silver mined in Peru and freighted by sea to the town of Panama, and also the treasure regularly brought by the Pacific galleons from the Philippines, not to mention the pearls which abounded in the seabed just off Panama itself. These caravans of gold, silver, gems and pearls were carried partly on horseback and partly by river northwards to the little port of Nombre de Dios, where, every January, a fleet from Spain would dock, take the priceless cargo aboard and return it to the royal treasuries in Seville and Madrid, where it would be used to finance the Spanish military power which dominated large parts of Europe. That fleet itself was a powerful one, immune from attack by pirates, however daring they might be, but Drake perceived that the weak link in this chain was the overland route across the Isthmus, and this became the target of his attention. For the best part of two years during the period 1569–71, Drake lived on this coast, raiding Spanish ships, exploring the interior, reconnoitring bases and bays, making contact with the *cimarrones*, and laying his plans. It is unlikely that Spain had a more patient and implacable enemy than this man, who seemed to regard his quest for personal vengeance as comparable with the workings of divine providence, saying:

*As there is a general vengeance which secretly pursueth the doers of wrong and suffereth them not to prosper, albeit no man of purpose empeach them, so is there a particular indignation, engraffed in the bosome of all that are wronged, which ceaseth not seeking by all means possible to redress or remedie the wrong received.*

By May 1572, Drake, now in his early thirties, was ready for a determined attempt on the Spanish treasure-route. With two small ships, the 40-ton *Swan* and the 70-ton *Pascha* (or *Pasco*) he sailed from Plymouth, now accompanied by two of his younger brothers, John and Joseph. After a swift Atlantic crossing, he moored in one of the secret coves just east of Nombre de Dios, which he had reconnoitred the year before. He named this place Port Pheasant, because of the abundance of game in the surrounding forests. Here Drake built a fortified stockade and unloaded three pinnaces which he had transported disassembled on board his ships. The pinnace was a small, shallow-draft boat with a single deck, which could be sailed or rowed into inlets or harbours, yet was large enough to hold two dozen men with their weapons and stores; with these boats Drake intended to launch stealth-attacks on his chosen targets. His first plan was stunningly audacious: with the three pinnaces he would take some seventy lightly armed men by night into the harbour of Nombre de Dios, and raid the treasure-house,

# Sir Francis Drake

## Reuiued :

## Calling vpon this Dull or Effeminate Age, to folowe his Noble Steps for Golde & Siluer,

By this Memorable Relation, of the Rare Occurrances
(neuer yet declared to the World) in a Third Voyage,
made by him into the West-Indies, in the Yeares 72. & 73.
when *Nombre de Dios* was by him and 52. others
only in his Company, surprised.

Faithfully taken out of the Reporte of Mr. *Christofer Ceely*, *Ellis
Hixon*, and others, who were in the same Voyage with him.
By *Philip Nichols*, Preacher.

Reviewed also by Sr. *Francis Drake* himselfe before his Death,
& Much holpen and enlarged, by diuers Notes, with his owne
hand here and there Inserted.

Set forth by Sr. *Francis Drake* Baronet
(his Nephew) now liuing.

AVXILIO DIVINO

SIC PARVIS MAGNA

## LONDON

Printed by *E. A.* for *Nicholas Bourne* dwelling at the
South Entrance of the *Royall Exchange*. 1626.

where he believed the precious cargo was stored, awaiting its transport to Spain.

The 'official' account of this raid given in Drake's nephew's book *Sir Francis Drake Revived* is not entirely clear or plausible, but it seems that, notwithstanding its bold simplicity, it ended in total failure. The boats did enter the harbour at the dead of night, but they were detected and the alarm was given. A sharp fight with local citizens ensued in the market square, which the English won at the cost of several casualties. They then approached the governor's house, and found huge heaps of silver bars, which Drake however refused to touch, telling his men that the treasure-house itself held a similar mountain of far more valuable gold and jewels. Leading them to its door, Drake ordered it to be broken open, but as he stepped forward 'his strength and sight and speech failed him, and he began to faint for want of blood … the blood filled the very prints which our footsteps made, to the great dismay of all our company, who thought it not credible that one man should be able to spare so much blood and live.' Presumably Drake had been wounded in the earlier fighting, but had given no sign of it. His frightened men then turned and carried their leader back to their boats and rowed away empty-handed. Why three or four men could not have attended to Drake, while the rest raided the defenceless treasure-house is a mystery. Perhaps this narrative was concocted to conceal the fact that Drake had mistimed his attack – carried out in late July, when the fleet bound for Spain had departed some weeks before and it is possible the treasure-house had already been emptied. If there was no gold, why did they then not go back for any of the huge mass of silver which they had seen in the governor's house?

Whatever the truth may be, the raiders were able to withdraw to Port Pheasant to rest and lay fresh plans. Apparently undaunted, Drake sailed east to the port of Cartagena (in modern Colombia), where he took several ships and looted their stores. He then put into operation a second part of his strategy, namely to forge an alliance with the *cimarrones*, with the aim of launching an overland attack on the treasure-train as it moved up from Panama. The negotiations with the *cimarrones* were successful, and they played a pivotal role in guiding Drake across the Isthmus, and reinforcing the fighting strength of his depleted party. Arriving back at his base, Drake was given the news that his younger brother John had died from wounds he had received while leading an attack on a passing ship. Only days afterwards, a large number of the men fell victim to a severe fever, and among those who died was Drake's second brother, Joseph. Drake's action following this double tragedy seems extraordinarily callous and unnecessary: he ordered the ship's surgeon to carry out a post-mortem to ascertain the cause of death. The surgeon reportedly found 'his liver swollen, his heart as it were sodden, the guts all fair', then he himself died of an infection contracted during this operation.

Drake now set out to march on Panama city, and if possible to seize one of the treasure shipments. Their route was steep and arduous, hacking through dense jungle and fording many rivers, and without the *cimarrones* the Englishmen could scarcely have succeeded in the tropical heat and the unknown terrain. This march has entered history for one particular episode: on a clear morning, the leader of *cimarrones* led Drake to an immense tree in which steps had been cut. Climbing to the top, Drake was astounded to see behind him to the north the Caribbean, while to the south his eyes rested on a great expanse of water which he knew to be the Pacific Ocean, hitherto sailed only by Spaniards and by one celebrated Portuguese, Magellan himself. According to the legend, Drake 'besought God of his goodness to give him leave and life to sail once in an English ship in that sea.' One of his colleagues, John Oxenham, 'protested that unless our Captain did beat

The Hondius portrait, undated but showing Drake aged forty-two. Probably engraved from life, Hondius's acquaintance with Drake enabled him also to produce his important map of the circumnavigation.
*British Museum*

him from his company, he would follow him by God's grace.' Oxenham was indeed to realise his dream, and before Drake, but the Pacific led Oxenham to tragedy and death, while it led Drake to glory.

While pressing on towards Panama, Drake learned from a *cimarron* spy sent on ahead that a convoy of mules laden with gold and jewels was indeed about to leave the city. An ambush was laid and, for the second time, Drake was within a hand's grasp of an immense treasure when one of their party, a drunken fool named Robert Pike, rushed forward prematurely and gave the alarm, sending the treasure convoy galloping back to Panama. Pike's punishment at Drake's hands is not recorded. There was no alternative but to return north and re-join their ships. By now it was February: they had been eight months on this tropical coast, exploring, planning, waiting and watching their comrades die of disease, and with no result. But somehow Drake succeeded in preserving discipline and morale among his men in the face of all these disappointments and dangers, which was no mean feat of leadership.

Their fortunes were about to change however. While Drake had been in the interior his men had captured a Spanish ship, well-laden with food and wine, on which they feasted and recovered their strength while the ship was retained for the homeward voyage. On 23 March 1573 the Englishmen were approached by a French ship, a privateer out of Le Havre, captained by Guillaume Le Testu (or Tetu). Le Testu was an interesting man – a Protestant, considerably older than

Sir Francis Walsingham, Queen
Elizabeth's private secretary from
1573–90. Far closer to Drake than Cecil
was, Walsingham certainly helped
Drake plan the Pacific expedition.
*National Portrait Gallery*

Drake (he was born around 1512),
he was a scholar and an experienced
seafarer, as well as being the author of
several important and artistic charts of
the Atlantic and the New World, which
still survive. At their first conference
he gave Drake the news of the
St Bartholomew's Day massacre in Paris
the previous summer, which can only
have intensified Drake's anti-Catholic
passions. Le Testu agreed to join forces
with Drake in a fresh attempt to
ambush the treasure from Panama, as
Drake's own resources in fighting men
had dwindled considerably.

The French and English raiders were landed close to Nombre de Dios, and
instructions were given to the pinnaces to return four days later to pick them up
again. Once again the *cimarrones* brought news of the approaching caravan; it was
massive, with almost 200 mules, each carrying up to 300 pounds in silver, totalling
in all nearly thirty tons. This time the ambush succeeded: after a brief fight, the
Spanish escort fled, leaving the treasure in the hands of Drake, Le Testu and their
men. All was not over however, for Le Testu had been wounded, and the guards
would certainly make for Nombre de Dios to fetch help. It was decided to bury
much of the silver for possible recovery later, and to make off with as much as
could be carried, back to the rendezvous with the pinnaces. Why they did not
simply lead away the mules still laden with the whole treasure is not clear;

perhaps the mules could not penetrate the dense forest. As the raiders struggled away through the jungle, now pursued by the Spanish, the unfortunate Le Testu fell behind, was captured and killed on the spot, and his head was later exhibited in the town market place.

Reaching the coast, Drake and his men found with dismay that the pinnaces were nowhere to be seen. They had either to await the arrival of the Spanish and fight, or find an escape route. Once again Drake showed his utter determination as he ordered a raft to be built from the abundant driftwood that came down in the numerous rivers from the interior. Trunks were lashed together, and a crude mast, sail and rudder were added. It was a brilliant piece of improvisation, and somehow they succeeded in sailing along the coast for six hours until they were at last rewarded by the sight of the pinnaces. They beached together and Drake exultantly revealed the captured treasure. The following day they made their way back to the *Pascha*, the captured ship and Le Testu's vessel, but Drake would not sail at once for England. Instead, he insisted on mounting a foray back into the jungle to rescue Le Testu and recover more of the silver; they were too late to help Le Testu, and the Spanish had also found some of the buried silver. Drake rewarded the *cimarrones* with gifts from his ships, for the treasure was of little interest to them, then at last satisfied, he set his course for home.

The story is that the men arrived back in Plymouth on Sunday 9 August, 1573, after an absence of almost fifteen months, during which they had been given up for dead. News of their return spread like wildfire through the town, reaching even the congregation in the church, 'so that few or none remained with the preacher, all hastening to see the evidence of God's love and blessing towards our gracious queen and country by the fruit of our Captain's labour and success.' Even after dividing the treasure with the French sailors and with his own crew, Drake was now a made man, one of the wealthiest commoners in the land, and a man whose fame extended well beyond England. The foundations of his legend had been laid and in the Spanish reports of these events, 'Drake the pirate' was singled out for special attention and warning, and it seems a strange and fitting coincidence that in Spanish his name means 'dragon'. In New Spain itself there was deep unease, and the council of the city of Panama pleaded with King Philip II of Spain to strengthen his colonies:

*The realm is at the present moment so terrified and the spirits of all so disturbed that we know not in what words to emphasise to your majesty the solicitude we make in this dispatch, for we certainly believe that if remedy be delayed, disaster is imminent. These English have so shamelessly opened the door and the way by which with impunity, wherever they desire, they will attack the pack-trains travelling overland.*

However, even Drake's thirst for revenge was satisfied, for the present at least, for several years passed before he sailed out once again into Spanish waters. We know a little about how he was occupied during those years. He bought property in Plymouth, and built more ships, which he hired out for commercial purposes. Perhaps Drake had ambitions to join the ranks of the great and powerful in Elizabethan society; certainly his next seafaring venture was as a member of a political and military campaign very different from his private raids on the Spanish Main. In 1574 he was enlisted by the Earl of Essex to provide a naval element in Essex's scheme to occupy Northern Ireland. Essex had Queen Elizabeth's blessing to take a private army to Ireland and to settle and govern the Antrim region, as part of the Elizabethan policy of enforcing English rule over the country. A part of Essex's plan was to take Rathlin Island, off the northern coast of Antrim, and fortify it as a military stronghold, and for this he approached Drake for his ships and his expertise. During the summer of 1575 Drake, using his own ships and others commandeered locally, assisted Essex and his chief officer, Captain John Norris, in the siege of Rathlin.

Whether Drake himself took part in the bloody battle and subsequent massacre of the defenders is unknown, and it seems doubtful that Drake received much financial reward for his services. What he did achieve was to make the acquaintance of a number of political and military figures of the time, and he himself became numbered among them. It has been plausibly argued that this was his motive in this Irish campaign – to gain entry into the circles of power that revolved around the queen and the court, to prepare the ground for future overseas adventures of a very ambitious kind. If this was so, then Drake succeeded, for he was, after 1575, counted one of the leading figures of his age in nautical matters. He had come an immense distance in the ten years since he had shipped as a common seaman with Hawkins's trading ventures. He was now thirty-five years old, wealthy, famous locally, and with connections in the nation's councils of power. He was self-confident and ambitious, but the shadow of Spain across Europe still irked him deeply. In Drake's mind, the idea was germinating for a new adventure, more dramatic and daring than ever before, and of a kind that no other man would even conceive.

2

The raiding of ports and treasure-ships was clearly the principal aim of the voyage.

# To the fearful strait 1577–78

At an unknown date early in 1577, a meeting took place between Drake and Queen Elizabeth that signalled the start of Drake's greatest achievement – his circumnavigation of the world. Perhaps the strangest thing about this historic adventure is that we do not know whether Drake deliberately set out to sail around the world, or whether it happened, in effect, by accident. In a speech made by Drake to his crew during the voyage – made to emphasise his royal authority – it became quite clear that the expedition was planned as part of the unofficial guerrilla war which the English government and people were eager to pursue against Spain.

*… the next day coming to her [Queen Elizabeth's] presence, these or the like words she said: Drake, so it is that I would gladly be revenged on the king of Spain for divers injuries that I have received; and said further that he [Drake] was the only man that might do this exploit, and withal craved his advice therein. Who told her Majesty of the small good that was to be done in Spain, but the only way was to annoy him by his Indies …*

We do not know whether it was before or after this interview that Drake conceived his master plan of entering the Pacific via the Straits of Magellan, and attacking the Spanish colonies from Chile northwards to the eastern seaboard of Mexico, which he correctly guessed would be virtually undefended, since none but Spanish ships ever sailed in these waters. The raiding of ports and treasure-ships was clearly the principal aim of the voyage. But the matter would become more complex than this, from a seafaring point of view, because the crucial question of the route back to England from the eastern Pacific remained to be decided. Drake's circumnavigation of the globe was his answer to that problem.

The 1570s had seen an upsurge in England's attempts to secure for herself a share in world trade, ideally her own routes to the East. As early as 1527, the

... the southe sea then
... to the northward, as
... alonge the same coaste a
... of the other to ... two
... have ..., so the ...
... this ... in a realme ...
... are not under the obedience of
... so is the greate hope of
... ..., ... ..., ... and
... commodities ... as maye
... ... money ...., and also
... ... greatly ...
... vp as a ... ... in to very ...
... southe sea ... yf he shalbe ...
... the fore named ... coaste, to ...
...) then he is to returne the same way
... as he went in. ... and ...
... your favor is to be ... in ... must
... though he ... from ... to ... in
... ... the coaste to gett ...
... the ... and commodities ...

... ... of this cause must be ... to
... otherwise the ... cannot ...
that your effort, as is ... ...

Previous page: The half-burned plan of
the circumnavigation, with its
ambiguous wording apparently
authorising Drake to explore the Pacific
coast of South America, but to return
the same way as he went.
*The British Library, Cott. Otho EVIII, f.9*

geographer Robert Thorne had written 'There is one way to discover, which
is into the north, for out of Spain they have discovered all the Indies and seas
occidental, and out of Portingall all the Indies and seas oriental.' From this theory
was born the dual quest for the north-east and north-west passages, for map-
makers, seamen and statesmen were all prepared to be convinced that beyond the
land masses of Asia and America, there must exist sea routes linking the Atlantic
and the Pacific Oceans. In this belief of course they were technically correct,
but in the sixteenth century no one understood that these routes were, for all
practical purposes, quite unnavigable, and the northern passages became the
object of repeated assaults by English mariners and their backers, who hoped
that success there would secure them a maritime monopoly to rival those of
Spain and Portugal.

This quest for an English route to the East, and the fact that Drake did
undoubtedly return via the Spice Islands, has given rise to the belief that the
Pacific crossing was the aim of the voyage from the outset, but there is really no
evidence for this: it was merely one of three possible routes by which his fleet
could return home. The first was simply to retrace his passage through the Straits
of Magellan into the South Atlantic; the second was via the Pacific; about the
third there has also been a great deal of speculation, namely that Drake would
search for and attempt the North-West Passage in reverse – from the northern
Pacific to the Atlantic via the 'Strait of Anian', which geographers imagined to
exist, separating Asia from America. This strait was placed on sixteenth-century
maps at roughly the place where the Bering Strait lies, but no European mariner
had ever seen it: it was a purely theoretical entity, a lucky guess, which was later
proved to be correct. Drake was certainly aware of the 'Strait of Anian' concept,
and he may indeed have kept it in his mind as one possible return route. One

final additional motive for his Pacific voyage has occasionally been suggested, namely that he was to search for *Terra Australis*, the great southern continent, which most geographers believed must exist to counterbalance all the earth's northern land masses. Most world maps of the sixteenth century show this huge, imaginary continent filling the southern portion of the globe; the land south of the Magellan Strait – named by Magellan Tierra del Fuego for its volcanoes – was commonly supposed to be the only known part of this *Terra Australis*.

Although the passage cited above gives no geographical details, a memorandum, sent either from or to Sir Francis Walsingham, Queen Elizabeth's principal secretary, has survived to give us an outline of Drake's royal commission. This document has been partly burned away, but enough has survived to convey the general intention. With the conjectural insertion of some of the lost words and phrases, the document reads:

41

*... enter the Strait of Magellanas lying in 52 degrees of the pole, and having passed*
*therefrom into the South Sea then he is to sail so far to the northward as 30 degrees,*
*seeking along the said coast ... to find out places meet to have traffic for the venting*
*of commodities of these her Majesty's realms. Whereas at present they are not under*
*the obedience of any Christian prince, so there is great hope of gold, silver, spices, drugs,*
*cochineal, and divers other special commodities, such as may enrich her Highness'*
*dominions, and also put shipping a-work greatly. And having gotten up as aforesaid in the*
*30 degrees in the South Sea (if it shall be thought meet by the afore named Francis Drake*
*to proceed so far) then he is to return by the same way homewards as he went out. Which*
*voyaging is by God's favour to be performed in 13 months, although he should spend*
*5 months in tarrying upon the coasts, to get knowledge of the princes and countries there.'*

This is the only written commission that we know of and there is no mention
here of crossing the Pacific to the Spice Islands; no mention of the Strait of
Anian; no mention of the Southern Continent; but nor is there any mention of
attacking Spanish ships or colonies, as discussed in Drake's private meeting with
the queen. Evidently no one concerned wanted that part of the plan written
down, and if Spain protested, the queen and her ministers would certainly deny
that Drake had any official status. From his private meeting with the queen,
Drake understood that he was to do exactly what he had done five years before
on the Isthmus of Panama, only this time the queen and other high-ranking
investors were backing him in order to share the treasure. Those investors
included Walsingham himself, the Earls of Leicester and Lincoln, Sir Christopher
Hatton, Sir William Winter and John Hawkins. The queen's name does not appear
on the list of subscribers to the venture, but she gave the royal ship, the *Swallow*,
and its assessed value was her stake. Each subscriber would be paid a dividend

'... so there is great hope of gold, silver, spices, drugs, cochineal, and divers other special commodities, such as may enrich her Highness' dominions, and also put shipping a-work greatly.'

according to their investment in the normal business way. One oddity in the document is the supposition that on the eastern side of South America, the territory below thirty degrees south was not under Spanish jurisdiction. This must have been faulty intelligence, for there were ports and colonies, albeit small ones as far south as Valdivia, lying at forty degrees south. The idea that there might be independent 'princes and countries' in southern Chile, perhaps resembling the Inca and Aztec nations, but still unknown to the Spanish, is also far fetched.

This was not in fact the first English plan to gain a foothold in South America. In 1574 another Devon adventurer, Sir Richard Grenville, had proposed a fanciful scheme for colonising land around the Strait of Magellan in order to provide a base for English exploration into the Pacific. It was because this plan came to nothing that Grenville turned his attention to the search for the North-West Passage, and to colonising North America. But while Drake and his backers were laying their plans, another English venture into the Pacific was already under way. John Oxenham, the man who had sailed with Drake in 1572–73 and who had also seen the Pacific from the high tree north of Panama, had sailed from England in 1576, intending to fulfil the ambition that he and Drake had conceived of being the first Englishman to sail in the Pacific; in this Oxenham succeeded, but at the cost of his life. Arriving in the Isthmus, Oxenham concealed his ship and trekked overland across the watershed with his crew, his stores and his weapons, aided once again by the faithful *cimarrones*. He then built a small craft and sailed downstream into the Gulf of Panama, where he attacked some Spanish ships and obtained pearls from the islands. But Oxenham met with ill luck on the return trek and he and many of his crew were captured by the Spanish, taken to Lima where they were interrogated by the Inquisition and,

The *Golden Hind* as depicted on the
Hondius world map.
*The British Library, Maps M.T.6.a.2*

eventually, in 1580, executed. Drake knew that Oxenham had left on this voyage and when he himself reached the Pacific he picked up news of his compatriot's imprisonment; he considered possible ways to bargain for his release, but without success.

By the autumn of 1577, Drake was engaged in assembling his fleet and his crew. Five ships were being made ready. Drake's own flagship, the *Pelican*, became, when renamed the *Golden Hind*, the most famous ship in English history until eclipsed by Nelson's *Victory*. She was supposedly named in honour of the queen, for Elizabeth was fond of identifying herself with the pelican symbol, a bird which bled to feed its young, just as she nourished her subjects with her own vitality and self-sacrifice. The ship was rated somewhere between 100 and 150 tons, and was perhaps seventy feet long – not large even by the standards of the day. However she was as well armed as many larger ships, with eighteen guns and an arsenal of smaller weapons – muskets, pistols, fire-bombs, fire-pikes, as well as dozens of swords and bows; in spite of the innocuous-sounding trading commission cited above, the *Pelican* was in reality an out-and-out warship. She was accompanied by the *Elizabeth* at eighty tons, captained by John Wynter, the *Swan* at fifty tons, captained by John Chester, the *Marigold* at thirty tons, under John Thomas, and the *Christopher* (also known as the *Bark Benedict*) at a mere fifteen tons, commanded by Thomas Moone. Four

# THE WORLD
## Encompaſſed

By
### Sir FRANCIS DRAKE,

Being his next voyage to that to *Nombre*
*de Dios* formerly imprinted;

Carefully collected out of the notes of Maſter
FRANCIS FLETCHER *Preacher in this im-
ployment, and diuers others his followers in
the ſame* :

Offered now at laſt to publique view, both for the honour of
the actor, but eſpecially for the ſtirring vp of *heroick ſpirits,*
*to benefit their Countrie, and eternize their names*
*by like noble attempts.*

*LONDON,*
Printed for NICHOLAS BOVRNE
and are to be ſold at his ſhop at the
*Royall Exchange.* 1628.

Title page of *The World Encompassed*, 1628, the 'official' account of the circumnavigation, edited by Drake's nephew from the eyewitness journal of Francis Fletcher. *The British Library, G.6519*

pinnaces were carried in pieces, to be assembled as required.

Reports vary as to the number of men who sailed in this fleet: around 160 seemed to be the consensus. The *Swan* was the supply ship, and it would be normal in an expedition of this kind to reckon on breaking up one or more of the vessels en route, not least because the loss of many crewmen in combat or to disease was a near certainty. The crews included smiths, a shoemaker, an apothecary, a tailor, musicians to entertain and boys to wait on Drake, and a preacher named Francis Fletcher. It was Fletcher's detailed journal of the voyage that provided the basic source material for Nichols's book *The World Encompassed*. A number of other eyewitness accounts of the voyage also survived, notably that of John Cooke, which was more critical of Drake as a man and as a commander than Fletcher's was.

As was normal on this kind of voyage, in addition to the working seamen, a number of gentlemen also embarked, most of them friends or relatives of the investors. Among these were Drake's brother Thomas, and his cousin John; John Hawkins's nephew, William; Fletcher himself was Walsingham's nominee; John Wynter was the son of George Wynter, Clerk of the Queen's Ships; most important of all there was Thomas Doughty, whose role in the early part of the voyage was to be fraught with mystery and misfortune. Doughty had fought alongside Drake in the Irish campaign of 1574, and the two men had apparently become very friendly. Doughty was young, well-connected in London and at court, being especially close to Sir Christopher Hatton, later to become Lord Chancellor. Drake was accepted as the fleet commander, but socially Doughty and John Wynter were his superiors, though the three were said to be 'equal companions and friendly gentlemen' in this adventure. Doughty was accompanied by his brother, John, and a lawyer-friend named Leonard Vicary.

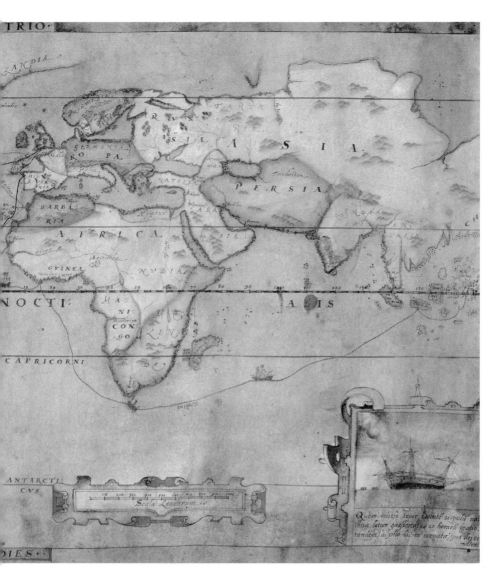

A matter of the greatest interest is the maps and charts which Drake carried
with him and used to plan the voyage, and on this we have some information.
He had one or two general printed world maps by Mercator and Ortelius, and
a large manuscript world map which he said he had obtained (how, we do not
know) from Lisbon, which may have been the work of Fernao Vaz Dourado,
the leading Portuguese chart-maker of his day. These maps would certainly have
located features such as the Magellan Strait and the Spice Islands, but only in the

most general way, and no captain of a later age would have cared to embark on such a voyage with only these maps as his guides. Drake was well aware that extreme caution was needed in coastal navigation, and where possible he commandeered local pilots, or sent ships' boats ahead of him in shoal waters. (Mariners of the sixteenth century seem to have had little fear of the open ocean, but what they did fear was the unknown coast, for to be caught on a hidden reef or sandbar meant disaster and death thousands of miles from all possible rescue.) In addition to his maps, Drake carried with him several books of navigation, including perhaps the English translation of Martin Cortes's *Art of Navigation*, and a copy of the narrative of Magellan's voyage. For his spiritual well-being he carried several Bibles (almost certainly copies of the 'Geneva Bible' with its dedication to Queen Elizabeth), Foxe's *Book of Martyrs*, from which he was inseparable, and the Psalms for singing with the crew.

After months of preparation the fleet was ready to sail from Plymouth on 15 November 1577, but severe storms forced their immediate return and a second start was made on 13 December. Officially the voyage had been publicised as a trading venture to the Mediterranean, but few people were convinced by this story and the Spanish ambassador in London was informed by his agents that this was a raiding party bound for New Spain. By early January, on the Moroccan coast, the piracy had already begun with the seizure of a forty-ton Spanish fishing vessel, which Drake exchanged for the little *Christopher*. Sailing on to the Cape Verde Islands, a second prize was taken, the large Portuguese merchantman, the *Santa Maria*. This vessel was laden with food and wine, but of more importance was that it was captained by Nuno da Silva, a man with expertise in South American pilotage, and Drake immediately commandeered both the ship and her captain.

Da Silva himself wrote his recollections of the voyage, which supplement in many important details the Fletcher narrative. It is from da Silva that we have the account of the maps and books that Drake carried, and also a striking description of Drake himself. Drake clearly impressed his Portuguese captive as an outstanding sea captain; dignified and courteous, but with huge strength of purpose. 'He is low in stature,' wrote da Silva, 'thickset and very robust. He has a fine countenance, is ruddy of complexion, and has a fair beard. He is a great mariner. He also read the psalms and preached.' Da Silva reported that he lived in great style, dining from silver dishes with his gentlemen friends, but that he led the religious services on deck with great fervour.

On leaving the Cape Verde Islands in early February the task before Drake, in maritime terms, was to sail south-west and raise the Brazilian coast as near as possible to Cape San Roque, and then proceed south until the Strait of Magellan was located around 52 degrees south; they hoped to rest and resupply before attempting the Strait. In the event, this portion of the voyage was to be wholly overshadowed by matters other than maritime navigation. As they left the islands, Drake appointed Thomas Doughty captain of the Portuguese ship, but very soon thereafter there began the long sequence of dissension and feuding between the two 'equal companions', which puzzled and divided the crew, and soured the entire following five months' sailing. Various incidents are reported in the eyewitness accounts of quarrels, insults, claim and counter-claim between Drake and Doughty and between their supporters, but the ultimate cause of this mysterious feud between two former friends has never been finally explained. Doughty was transferred to the *Swan*, the supply ship, and Drake began a campaign of deriding Doughty to his men, gathering evidence of his alleged misdeeds, and attempting to isolate him from the rest of the crew and from the gentlemen passengers.

By early April the fleet was sailing within sight of the Brazilian coast, and when the River Plate was reached, they anchored to take on fresh food and water. In bad weather the fleet of small boats had difficulty staying together, and one or other of the ships was often out of contact. At Rio Deseado, Drake decided to strip and abandon the *Swan*, thus depriving Doughty of any remaining command status. Drake was also putting about the rumour that Doughty was a necromancer, who had deliberately conjured the storms which beset them. A little further south, Drake determined to winter from mid-June onwards at Port San Julian, lying at 49 degrees south, which had also served as Magellan's winter quarters. Was it an omen that the gallows was still standing where the great pioneer had executed a group of mutineers almost sixty years before? For Drake had now determined to put an end to the feud with Doughty by putting him on trial for mutiny.

On 30 June 1578, all the men were assembled ashore and Drake, having had Doughty's arms bound, announced the intended trial. Doughty proclaimed himself willing to make his defence before a legal court in England, but Drake brushed this aside, swore in a jury and ordered a list of charges to be read out. These were taken from reports of various crew members to the effect that Doughty had for months been hindering Drake's command, and inciting the 'overthrow' of the voyage. One important additional matter also emerged now – Doughty let slip the fact that William Cecil, Lord Burghley, Queen Elizabeth's Lord Treasurer, had a map or plan of their voyage:

*No, that he hath not, quoth Master Drake. The other replied that he had. How? quoth Master Drake. He had it from me, quoth Master Doughty. Lo, my masters, quoth he [Drake], what this fellow hath done; God will have his treacheries all known, for her*

*Majesty gave me special commandment that of all men my Lord Treasurer should not know it, but see his own mouth hath betrayed him.*

The significance of this is that Cecil, the queen's leading advisor, was strongly opposed to antagonising Spain through such a raiding voyage as Drake was planning, and therefore the queen wished all knowledge of it to be kept from him – at least this was what Drake claimed. It is possible that Doughty was involved in some intrigue behind Drake's back, but, at all events, treachery against the queen, before even the commencement of the voyage, was now added to Doughty's charge. The gentlemen in the company were deeply unhappy with the way things were proceeding and Leonard Vicary, Doughty's lawyer friend protested that 'this is not law nor agreeable to justice'. But Drake was the dominant personality, the indispensable leader of the expedition, and the loyalty of the seamen was to him; the gentlemen were heavily outnumbered and there was little they could do. The jury probably had no suspicion that a death sentence was contemplated, and brought in a verdict of guilty. Drake then took aside a group of the gentlemen and leading seamen, and showed them a bundle of letters from his powerful patrons – from Walsingham, Essex, Hawkins and Hatton – which he claimed gave him supreme authority on all decisions to be made during the voyage. With an oath, Drake then claimed to have left in his cabin the most important document of all – the royal commission. Nevertheless he had sufficiently impressed his colleagues, and he asked them if they were prepared to risk the success of the entire voyage by allowing dissent and mutiny to spread among the crews. He then asked for a show of hands by those 'that think this man worthy to die'; no one dared oppose Drake, and Doughty's fate was sealed.

Doughty was given two days to prepare his soul for death. Strangely, he

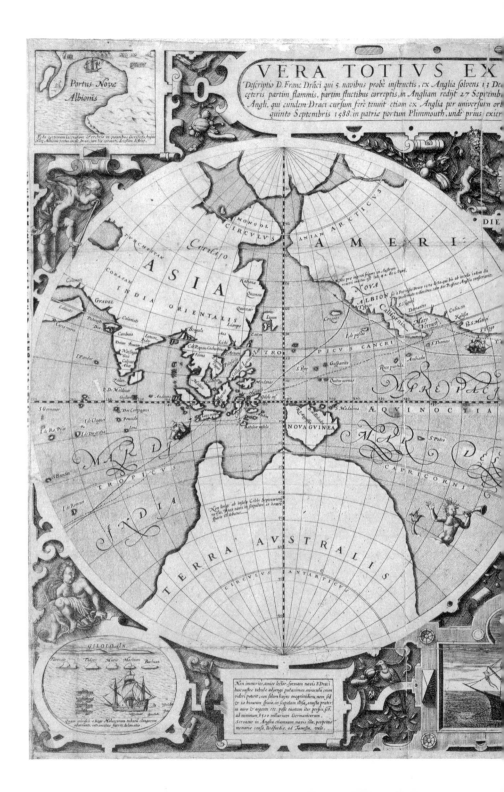

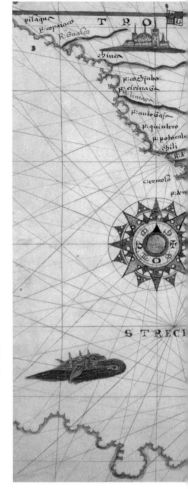

Previous page: The Hondius world map marking the circumnavigation. Since it refers also to the voyage of Cavendish, this undated map cannot be earlier than 1589. Less crude geographically than the van Sype map (see page 78), it probably has a closer personal link with Drake.
*The British Library, Maps M.T.6.a.2*

The Strait of Magellan depicted by the Catalan chart-maker Joan Martines at exactly the time of Drake's voyage. Its course is not shown with any degree of accuracy, and the land to the south was thought to be part of the mythical southern continent.
*The British Library, Harley MS 3450, f.12*

appeared in this time to become reconciled with Drake. They dined and took communion together, and, in the final moments, the condemned man embraced Drake and called him his 'good captain', before laying his neck upon the block and meeting his end. Drake at once held Doughty's head aloft and proclaimed him to have been a traitor, and to have met the end that awaits all traitors. Drake then addressed all his men with a powerful speech, calling for an end to dissension between the gentlemen and the mariners, which he implied had been the cause of all the trouble and of the planned mutiny:

*Thus it is, my masters, that we are very far from our country and friends, we are compassed in on every side with our enemies, wherefore we are not to make small reckoning of a man, for we can not have a man, if we would give for him ten thousand pounds. Wherefore we must have these mutinies and discords that are grown amongst us redressed, for by the life of God it doth even take my wits from me to think on it; here is such controversy between the sailors and the gentlemen, and such stomaching [resentment] between the gentlemen and the sailors, that it doth even make me mad to hear it. But my masters I must have it left, for I must have the gentleman to hail and draw with the mariner and the mariner with the gentleman. What, let us show ourselves to be all of a company, and let us not give occasion to the enemy to rejoice at our decay and overthrow.*

Drake then dismissed the captains and officers, and immediately reinstated them under his specific authority. Thus, partly through respect and partly through fear,

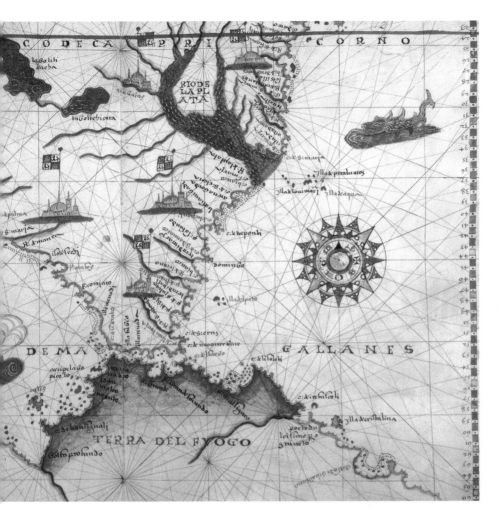

Drake asserted his command over the voyage and everyone on it. But a number of the gentlemen were deeply disturbed by what they had witnessed, and their feelings would surface later in the accounts which they gave of it after their return to England.

The execution of Thomas Doughty is, like the desertion of Hawkins at San Juan de Ulua, one of those problematic events in Drake's career which refuse to be explained away. No one else on the expedition appeared to feel that Doughty's actions seriously deserved death, yet Drake seemed passionately convinced that his own peace and security, and the success of the entire voyage hinged on the elimination of this man. Perhaps there was another, more personal motive at work in Drake's mind as just four years later, back in England, among those who knew Drake well, the rumour that Drake's wife Mary had once betrayed her husband with none other than Thomas Doughty began to circulate. Drake, so the rumour ran, had brilliantly contrived this act of legalised murder to take revenge on his former friend. This story is impossible to verify, but those who started it must have had some basis: Mary Drake and Doughty must at least have been acquainted and have spent time together for it to have been remotely credible. But perhaps there is another, simpler explanation, namely the tremendous strain – even on a man like Drake – of leading such a long, dangerous expedition into unknown waters, with his reputation or even his life as the price of failure. Who can say what the psychological effects of such a command would have been and whether the toll exacted itself in fear, loneliness and imagined offences? However, the story about Drake's wife and the story about the plan shown to William Cecil do serve one purpose: they remind us that this great voyage necessitated a long period of planning involving many figures, major and minor, and that during that period there may indeed have been discussions, intrigues, expectations or enmities of which we know nothing.

With this strange tragedy behind them, the mariners were now free to address themselves to the challenge ahead: the passage of Magellan's Strait. The captured Portuguese ship, the *Santa Maria*, was leaking badly, and was abandoned. The three remaining ships, the *Pelican*, the *Marigold*, and the *Elizabeth*, now made repairs and took on board what supplies they could before leaving Port San Julian. Then, heading south, the little fleet soon found itself, on 23 August 1578, in near-Antarctic waters at the mouth of the Strait. This passage, which would not be accurately charted until the early nineteenth century, even today retains a fearsome reputation among seafarers: it is some 350 miles long, and between two and twenty miles wide; its overall course is west, then south, then sharply north-west. The Atlantic opening is broader and more clearly evident than that on the Pacific side, which is a maze of narrow channels. It is intensely cold, beset by fierce currents, storms and dense fogs, and much of the passage is overlooked by mountains and sheer cliffs, which offer no refuge to the mariner in an emergency.

In Drake's day this strait had been passed by only a handful of expeditions, all Spanish. Magellan himself took thirty-eight days to sail through it, and then a second Spanish voyage in 1525 captained by Garcia de Loyasa, ended with such a disastrous loss of ships and men that it was virtually ignored thereafter. The Spanish established an alternative route across the central Pacific to connect their Philippines colony with New Spain at Panama. It was Drake's unique originality and daring which enabled him to attempt the first non-Spanish passage of this forbidding sea route. No detailed charts of it were available and no one in the fleet, even the captive Portuguese pilot, Nuno da Silva, had any experience of it. The reports of the English mariners confirmed the received legend concerning the inhabitants of this region – that they were of gigantic stature, and of a savage disposition. This latter they attributed to the brutal treatment which they had received years ago at the hands of the Spaniards: 'The Spanish cruelties have made them more monstrous in mind and manners than they are in body … for the loss of their friends, the remembrance whereof is assigned and conveyed over from one generation to another, breedeth an old grudge.' Before entering the Strait, Drake held a brief shipboard ceremony reminding the crews of their duty to Queen Elizabeth, during the course of which he renamed his flagship the *Pelican* as the *Golden Hind*, in honour of Sir Christopher Hatton, whose coat of arms displayed a golden deer.

In the event, Drake's fleet had unusually good weather, for they managed
to complete the passage of the Strait in just fourteen days, despite cautious sailing,
in which boats were sent ahead of the main ships, taking repeated soundings and
examining the various channels. About one third of the way through the Strait,
the Englishmen reconnoitred three islands, where they killed hundreds of
penguins to replenish their food stocks. They thought these islands sufficiently
'fair and large and fruitful' to claim formal possession of them for the queen,
naming the largest of them Elizabeth Island. However, when the ships emerged
thankfully into the Pacific on 6 September, their fortunes changed dramatically.
For some days they held a course north-west, for all the extant maps showed the
coast of South America to lie in that direction, but they found only open sea, and
were suddenly overtaken by a ferocious storm which all but destroyed the whole

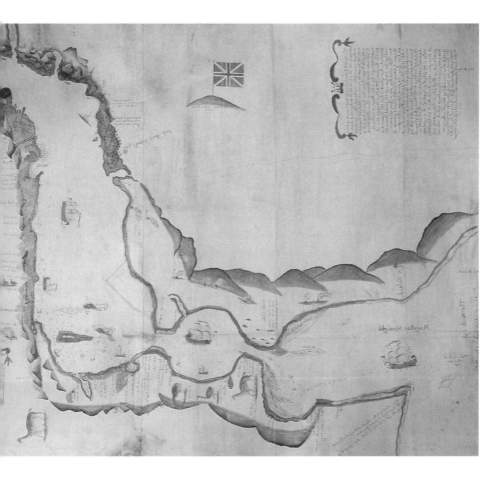

enterprise. A savage wind sprang up from the north and blew without mercy day after day, so that the tiny vessels could only run before it surrounded by the mountainous seas. In this tempest the *Marigold* disappeared entirely with all her crew, unseen by the other ships, although the *Golden Hind* and the *Elizabeth* somehow remained in contact with each other. After two weeks of this battering, the wind eased and shifted into the south, enabling the crews to sail back to the western entrance of the Strait once more. But the respite proved brief, and before they could succeed in landing and recuperating, a fresh storm arose again from the north.

This time John Wynter managed to steer the *Marigold* into shelter in the mouth of the Strait, while Drake and the *Golden Hind* were driven far to the south. There now occurred the most important geographical discovery of the

Previous page: A later and far more
accurate chart of the Magellan Strait,
drawn in 1670 by the English navigator
John Narborough. South is at the top.
Lacking a chart like this, Drake was
compelled to send boats ahead of his
ships to take soundings and search for
hidden reefs.
*The British Library, Maps K.Top. CXXIV.84*

entire voyage as the ship was reportedly hurled as far as 56 degrees south and east 'towards the Pole Antarctic as a pelican alone in the wilderness … with the most mad seas, the lee shores the dangerous rocks, the contrary and most intolerable winds, the most impossible passage out.' Drake felt sure that he had in fact passed Tierra del Fuego, and that this land was no part of *Terra Australis*, that he had reached 'the uttermost cape of headland of all these islands', which he thought 'stands near in 56 degrees, without [beyond] which there is no main or island to be seen to the Southwards, but the Atlantic Ocean and the South Sea meet in a most large and free scope.' We cannot say that Drake discovered the Cape Horn route, for we cannot be sure whether Drake was actually close to Horn Island itself, or perhaps Isle Hermite or Hardy Peninsula, but it is certain that Drake was able to refute the myth that the Magellan Strait offered the only passage between the Atlantic and Pacific Oceans, and to show that an open sea route existed a little further to the south. Appropriately this passage is now named after Drake.

Naturally, at the time, Drake was more concerned with survival and with the rescue of his expedition than with geographical innovation. An easing of the storms at last allowed him to shape a northerly course once more and attempt to rendezvous with the *Marigold*. This was impossible however as John Wynter, having waited in the Magellan Strait for several weeks in the hope that his commander would join him, reluctantly took the decision to return to England, believing himself the sole survivor of the fleet. He toyed with the idea of attempting the Pacific crossing, but his crew had no heart for it; had they agreed, perhaps Wynter's name might now be almost as famous as Drake's own. Wynter struggled back to England but later, when Drake had in effect come back from dead, he would face charges of deserting his leader. A strong presumption that he had acted responsibly in a life-or-death situation prevailed, however, and he was

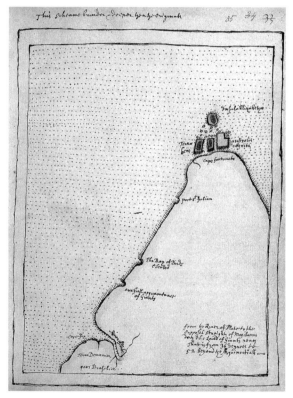

spared any punishment. Meanwhile Drake had realised that the existing maps were wrong in showing the South American coast trending to the north-west and so he sailed due north and intercepted the rugged, icy and heavily indented continental coastline. As soon as he was able, he landed to find food and rest his men before heading north as rapidly as possible into warmer latitudes, and on 25 November they reached the small island of Mocha, in 38 degrees south, just north-west of the port of Valdivia. Here, however, they were fiercely attacked by the Indian inhabitants and several men were killed and wounded, with Drake himself narrowly escaping being blinded by an arrow in his face. In spite of this, the author of *The World Encompassed* was strangely enthusiastic about the idea of colonising the region, claiming that the island was rich in gold and would provide a stepping stone to conquests on the mainland, but Drake had little interest in such schemes.

# 3

# An Englishman in the Pacific 1578–85

Drake had now gained the Pacific Ocean. He had survived almost a year of tremendous trials, physical and psychological, and while his crew's strength was reduced (he now commanded fewer than eighty men aboard one ship) he was well armed. Perhaps he still believed it possible that the *Elizabeth* would re-join him, but the fact remained that the Spanish had no idea that an English warship was loose in their territory and thus he could begin doing what he did best – piracy and plunder, achieved through the surprise attack. The first target port was the little town of Valparaiso, where the English raiders easily captured a sizeable ship, the *Capitana*, then ransacked the town, seizing from both food, wine and valuables. Perhaps the most practical item found there was a Spanish pilot book, a compendium of sailing directions for the western coast of South America, containing information unknown except to Spanish navigators. Moving north, Drake beached for several weeks in a deserted bay to clean his ships, build the pinnaces he had brought for reconnaissance, and unload additional cannon which had been stowed in the hold. He then set out to 'make' his voyage by plundering at will. He had nothing to fear from enemy ships, for all the Spanish vessels in the Pacific were unarmed merchantmen. Some of the ports housed moderate garrisons, but others were all too vulnerable.

From December 1578 to April 1579, along the coast of northern Chile and Peru and thence into the waters off eastern Mexico, Drake took ships and plundered towns, to the amazement of the dismayed Spaniards who had imagined this coast to be immune from attack. Among other things, Drake also picked up information from those temporarily held captive, and he learned that John Oxenham and some of his men were at that moment lying in the dungeons of Lima. He meditated a possible plan to ransom them, but it proved impracticable. He also heard rumours of a richly laden treasure-ship, which had only recently

Caca Fogo.

Caca Plata.

sailed out of Lima, making for Panama and the cross-country shipment route.
Drake immediately decided to pursue her northwards. For five hundred miles,
from Callao to the Gulf of Guayaquil, they coasted with all speed, pausing briefly
to plunder other ships en route. (In some of these attacks Drake employed more
force than usual, threatening his captives with death and preparing mock
executions to force them to reveal their treasure cargoes, but, in general, Drake
did not engage in gratuitous brutality towards his enemies or his prisoners.)
When he was almost exactly on the equator, just two days' sail from Panama, at
last the prize-ship was sighted and, after a brief hand-to-hand skirmish, Drake's
men boarded her and shut her crew in the cabins. The ship was officially named
*Nuestra Senora de la Concepcion*, but she was nicknamed *Cacafuego*, meaning
something like 'Spitfire', and she carried a treasure whose value has been
calculated at around £125,000 in Elizabethan money – many millions in modern
terms. Six days were needed to examine it and transfer it to the *Golden Hind*,
before the ship and her crew were released unharmed. The captain of the ship,
San Juan de Anton, later wrote an account of this dramatic encounter with
Drake, mentioning that Drake had displayed before him a large manuscript world
map, and had discussed with him his possible routes home. Drake also handed
Anton a written warning concerning the English prisoners in Lima, threatening
to kill thousands of Spaniards if they were not released.

Drake was in excellent humour; his voyage was made if he could but return
to England with his magnificent treasure. But how was he to do this? He guessed
that the news of his raids would have spread like wildfire through the colonies,
and would soon reach Spain itself. If he took the route which he knew – back
through the Magellan Strait, there was the very real danger that the Spanish
would try to intercept him at some point, and moreover the currents around the

entire coast of South America were adverse for such a course. There remained the Pacific crossing or the fabled 'Strait of Anian'. On one of his prizes, Drake had actually captured a navigator who knew the Pacific route to the Philippines and thence to the Moluccas (in modern Malaysia). Drake attempted, by bribery and uncharacteristic brutal treatment (including stringing the man up until he lost consciousness) to induce him to pilot the *Golden Hind* to the East Indies, but the man stoutly refused.

However, from this ship Drake acquired further charts and sailing directions, which gave him valuable information on the northern Pacific and the Californian coast. This ship, whose name is not recorded, was retained alongside the *Golden Hind* until the moment when the Pacific crossing was commenced and, soon afterwards, Drake took yet another Spanish ship, laden not with gold but with silks and fine China. This episode is of interest because among those on board was a nobleman named Don Francisco de Zarate, who, like Captain Anton before him, left a rather vivid picture of Drake as a man and a commander. Zarate was obviously in awe of the celebrated English avenger, and Drake played up to him, casting himself in the role of gentleman-thief. Drake invited Zarate to dine with him from his finest plate, which he boasted was a gift from the queen, showered him with presents (from goods which he had stolen), and then released him unharmed. Anton and Zarate both contributed to something resembling a personality cult of Drake, which flourished even among some of the Spanish themselves and which depicted him as daring, dignified and magnanimous, an adversary worthy of their own traditions of honour. Zarate noticed however that Drake's men seemed in considerable fear of him, and that he punished the least fault severely. Perhaps this was the memory of the Doughty episode still vivid in their minds.

At Guatulco on the Mexican coast just south of Acapulco, Drake landed in mid April, pillaged the town fairly comprehensively, and took on enough water for a fifty-day voyage, suggesting that he was still pondering the Pacific crossing (which, as he knew from his captured Spanish sailing directions, began from Acapulco). At Guatulco, too, he finally released Nuno da Silva, the Portuguese pilot who had served with him for more than a year, and who unexpectedly found through Drake, a small place in history. As a result, da Silva was able to discuss with the Spanish authorities the all-consuming problem of Drake's route home and throughout April and May the Spanish fully expected Drake to arrive in Acapulco, where they hoped that they might attack him and avenge themselves. But the weeks passed, and he did not appear, and in fact he was never seen again on the eastern coast of New Spain. He had sailed north-west, towards California, and it seems possible that he really was curious to see if the 'Strait of Anian' truly existed. Had he not after all passed triumphantly through the feared Strait of Magellan? Why should not an equivalent strait of no great length exist at the opposite extreme of the Americas, and why should it not yield also to his audacity? There was one other possible, and more practical, reason for sailing north – the season was not right for the Pacific crossing. Drake would have learned from his Spanish sources that the autumn was the favourable time for the easterly winds to take him to the Moluccas, so perhaps he planned to rest for two summer months on the North American coast, well out of reach of the Spaniards, and then set out westwards across the Pacific. At all events, he turned his back on the coastline where he was watched for, and spent several days cruising west-north-west, before once again turning due north to intercept the Californian coast. It was on this coast that there occurred perhaps the most intriguing and eternally debated episode of this entire voyage: the founding of 'New Albion'.

The Hondius map: the all-important vignette of 'Nova Albion'. This, the only visual clue to the mysterious bay, has led generations of researchers to favour Drake's Bay, north of San Francisco, as the likely site of Drake's anchorage. *The British Library, Maps M.T.6.a.2*

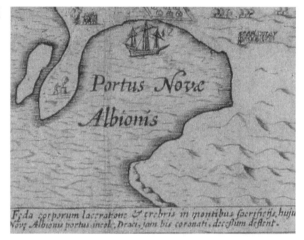

Like all good historical stories, that of Drake's visit to California has thrived on its mysteries. The 'official' version given in *The World Encompassed* is that Drake's two ships sailed for some 2,500 miles along the Californian coast, seeking the 'Strait of Anian'. Finally, reaching a latitude of 48 degrees, where they encountered bitingly cold weather, and still 'a large sea trending to the north', they turned back. If this is true, they would have been barely a day's sail from the entrance to Juan de la Fuca Strait, which they would surely have explored, believing it to be the 'Strait of Anian'. There are reasons though for doubting this account. Firstly, other narratives, such as the one Hakluyt published around 1595 from supposedly authentic sources, gave significantly different latitudes; Hakluyt says that 43 degrees was the most northerly point. Secondly, there are the graphic descriptions of the arctic conditions experienced between 42 and 48 degrees north: ice forming on the rigging in the bitter cold, food freezing the moment it was removed from the fire, exposure and hypothermia among the crew. Are such conditions credible in mid-June on the coasts of the modern states of Oregon and Washington, or were they embroidered to justify abandoning the search for the northern strait? The narrator argued strongly that the 'Strait of Anian' myth was now exploded:

*... either there is no passage at all through these northern coasts (which is most likely) or if there be, that yet it is unnavigable. Add hereunto that though we searched the coast diligently ... yet found we not the land to trend so much as one point in any place towards the east, but rather running on continually north-west, as if it went directly to meet with Asia; ... we had a smooth and calm sea, with ordinary flowing and reflowing, which could not have been had there been a frete [strait]; of which we rather infallibly concluded than conjectured, that there was none.*

So Drake's decision as to his homeward route was made for him: he must cross the Pacific, but first he must resupply and clean his ships, for which he needed a safe harbour. According to the official version once again, the ships made southwards to 38 degrees north, where they found just the anchorage they were looking for – a sheltered bay overlooked by white cliffs, offering fresh water and game for food, and inhabited by Indians who were welcoming and subservient. Here Drake and his crew remained for five weeks, from 17 June to 23 July 1579, and here, according to the narrative, he founded the territory of *Nova Albion*, a name inspired partly by the white cliffs. The Englishmen landed and camped, and at once built themselves a defensive stone wall, which proved unnecessary since the Indians seemed overawed by their strange guests. Each day they brought gifts and food to them, and attempted to communicate with them. Their obviously conciliatory speeches were interpreted by the visitors as offering total obedience to their will, and led to a ceremony in which Drake was effectively crowned King Regent to Queen Elizabeth:

*... they would resign unto him their right and title in the whole land, and become his vassal in themselves and their posterities...because they were not only visited of the gods (for so they still judged us to be) but the great and chief God was now become their God,*

*their king and patron … wherefore in the name and to the use of her most excellent*
*majesty, he [Drake] took the sceptre, crown and dignity of the said country into his hand;*
*wishing … especially that so tractable and loving a people as they showed themselves to be,*
*might have means to have manifested their most willing obedience the more unto her, and*
*by her means as a mother and nurse to the church of Christ, might by the preaching of the*
*gospel, be brought to the right knowledge and obedience of the true and ever-living God.*

70

MEN BY THESE PRESENTS
579.

AND IN THE NAME OF HER
OF ENGLAND AND HERR
E POSSESSION OF THIS
SO ILE FREELY RESIGNE
HOLE LAND VNTO HERR
NED BY ME AND TO BEE
VS ALBION.

DRAKE.

Previous page: The notorious 'Plate of
Brass' reportedly set up by Drake to
mark the founding of the colony of *Nova
Albion*. This artefact was found near
Drake's Bay in 1937, and generated
huge controversy; it is now considered
to be a forgery.
*Courtesy of the Bancroft Library,
University of California, Berkeley*

This is the language of European politics, sovereignty, fealty, imperialism and
religious zeal, which can have meant absolutely nothing to the Indians whom Drake
encountered here. If the 'Strait of Anian' did not exist, the possibility of placing
a colony here, on the very borders of the Spanish territories, was remote. Nevertheless, this ceremony was a move in the imperial game, which might one day
prove useful. To commemorate it, the Englishmen set up the famous plate of brass

*... nailed upon a fair great post, whereupon was engraven her Majesty's name, the day
and year of our arrival there, with the free giving up of the province and people into her
Majesty's hands, together with her Highness' picture and arms, in a piece of sixpence
of current English money under the plate, whereunder was also written the name of
our general.*

But where did all this take place? Where was *Nova Albion*? Enthusiastic scholars
have argued for at least six possible sites, lying close to 38 degrees north, that is,
somewhere very close to San Francisco Bay, while sceptics have dismissed all the
latitude data as so contradictory and unreliable that no site can ever be positively
identified. One of the plainest clues, the realistic-looking little vignette on the
Hondius world map of 1596, which claims to show *Portus Nova Albionis*, has
been dismissed as geographically worthless; yet this sketch has helped to favour
the strongest claimant – Drake's Bay, immediately north of San Francisco.
This bay received its name only in modern times, but its location and physical
character best fit the traditional accounts that we have of *Nova Albion*. Its case
was probably not helped by the discovery there in 1937 of the celebrated 'plate
of brass' itself, much studied and passionately argued over, but now regarded
as a modern forgery.

So Drake's voyage to California retains its mystery and we don't know whether he seriously searched for the 'Strait of Anian' or whether he almost discovered Vancouver Island. We can't say for sure if he camped for a month or more near San Francisco or whether he and his contemporaries believed that they had established a serious British claim to territories in North America. All this has been strongly debated for a century and more, and, despite various claims to have found the final answer, there is no sign that the debate will ever end. Like the fate of the Princes in the Tower, or the identity of the Man in the Iron Mask, the attempt to locate *Nova Albion* remains irresistible to those addicted to historical puzzles. This controversy has recently been revived by the radical claim that Drake sailed much further north than previously thought, as far as Chatham Strait at 57 degrees north, exploring Vancouver Island en route. This claim is based on very slender evidence, and the theory of a subsequent concealment seems strained and implausible: what was Drake concealing, since no 'Strait of Anian' had been discovered, and no other English fleet ever returned to that coast to exploit whatever Drake was supposed to have found?

By the end of July 1579, Drake had scrapped the captured Spanish chart ship and was ready to leave the North American coast with the *Golden Hind* alone to face the challenge of the Pacific. If he could overcome it, he knew that he would arrive in England a made man, with riches to spare for the rest of his life. But he knew this dream was still more than a year away, and he did not underestimate the dangers ahead: having survived some 5,000 miles of ocean, he must thread his way through the complex maze of the East Indian islands, menaced by both the Portuguese and the local Islamic rulers. It was a daunting prospect for a man in a single ship with a king's fortune lying in the hold.

From the end of July until end of September, the *Golden Hind* pressed steadily south-west and then west, keeping a course around 10 degrees north,

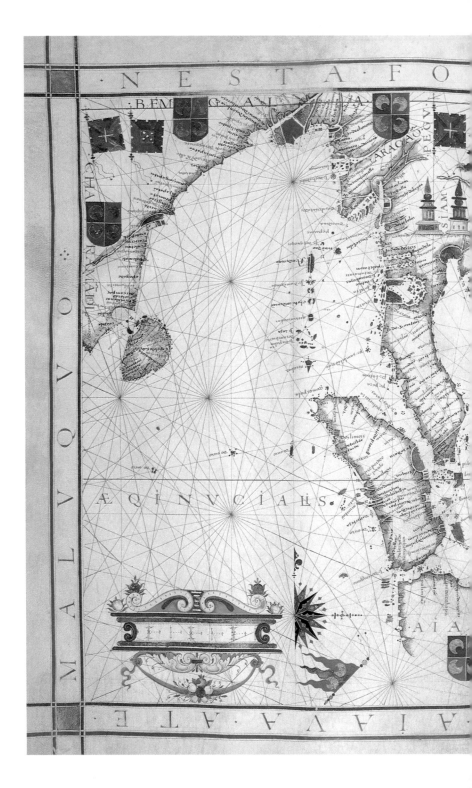

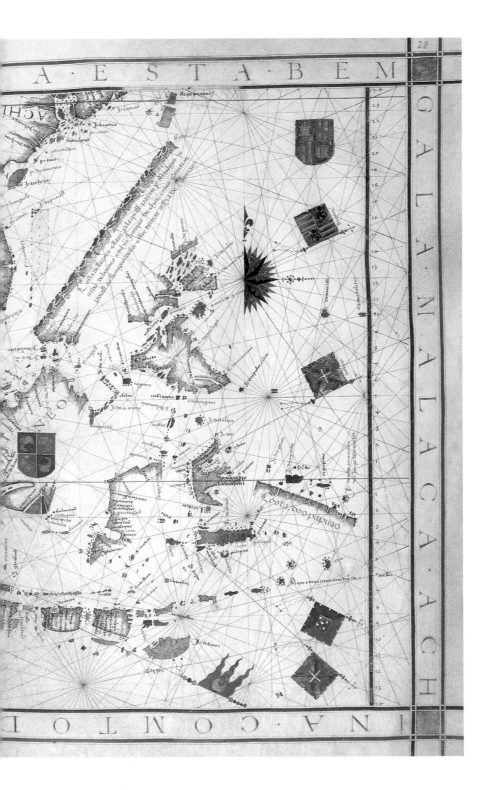

cruising with the northern equatorial current. This part of the voyage was uneventful, but a number of island groups were missed before the first landfall in more than sixty days was made on some unidentified islands in 8 degrees north and still some way east of the Philippines. Here food and water were obtained, but the natives who swarmed around them in their canoes proved so troublesome that the Englishmen hastened away from the place they christened the 'Island of Thieves'; whether this was the *Ladrones* where Magellan had also landed is impossible to say. They sailed on to Mindanao before turning south to cruise through the Moluccas, the fabled 'Spice Islands' themselves. At the little island of Ternate Drake was welcomed by the Moslem Sultan, who had apparently no love for the Portuguese, and who grasped the chance to trade with an alternative European power. The *Golden Hind* was towed into harbour by a fleet of canoes amid much pageantry, music and exchanging of gifts, yet there was an under-current of suspicion on both sides, for the Sultan would not come aboard and Drake would not go ashore, so embassies were sent instead. By bartering a little of his treasure, Drake obtained six tons of cloves and ginger, then left Ternate, perhaps uncertain whether a worthwhile foothold in the eastern trade had been established, although follow-up voyages from England did take place in the 1580s.

They had not felt secure enough in Ternate to make a prolonged stay, so Drake now sought an uninhabited island where they might rest and recover from the Pacific passage. This they found at an unidentified place which they named Crab Island, and where food and water were abundant. Embarking once more on 12 December they had a difficult passage through the myriad channels and shoals east of Celebes, and it was here that disaster struck. On the night of 8–9 January 1580, the ship was edging gently through apparently open water, when:

The Hondius map: vignette of the *Golden Hind* aground on a reef off Celebes in January 1580, the moment when the great voyage came nearest to failure and disaster.
*The British Library, Maps M.T.6.a.2*

*... they ran suddenly on a rock where they stuck fast from eight of the clock at night till four the next day in the afternoon, they being out of all hope of getting off; but having in the mean space lighted their shop of three ton of cloves and two pieces of ordnance and certain meal and beans, they hoisted all the sails in their ship; the wind, which before came from the starboard side, now changing to the larboard side, blew a good gale and drove their ship off the rock on float again, whereof they were not a little joyful. But while they stuck fast on this rock, thinking there to have all perished, Master Fletcher their minister made them a sermon and they received the communion all together and then every thief reconciled himself to his fellow thief.*

What this account does not mention is that Fletcher's sermon called on all the men, Drake included, to repent their sins, and went on to suggest that the imminent wreck of the ship was divine retribution for the murder of Thomas Doughty. When the crisis had passed Drake had his revenge on Fletcher. Manacling him to a hatch cover, Drake struck him with his slipper and 'excommunicated' him, denouncing him 'to the devil and all his angels'. Finally Drake compelled Fletcher to wear on his arm for the rest of the voyage a placard that read 'Francis Fletcher, the falsest knave that liveth'.

The world map by Nicola van Sype commemorating the circumnavigation. This is a most enigmatic map, undated, signed by a map-maker about whom absolutely nothing is known, and displaying some bizarre geographical features, for example the claim that Greenland had been discovered by Drake. Different editions exist with text in French and Dutch, the former claiming to have been 'seen and corrected' by Drake himself. Whether it was a copy of the manuscript map presented to Queen Elizabeth can only be conjectured.
*The British Library, Maps C.2.a.7*

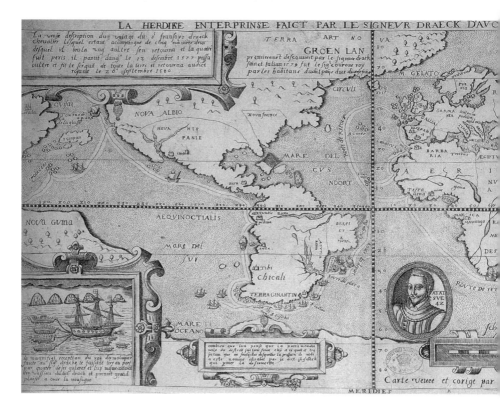

Because of the food they had been compelled to jettison, another halt was made in Java to restock, where the Englishmen paid highly for their supplies with more of their treasure. From Java, an uneventful voyage of two months took them to the Cape of Good Hope, and from there to Sierra Leone. From the Guinea coast they had to sail north-west to the Azores in order to pick up a favourable westerly wind for the final run to England. Drake's desperate hope now was to

TOVTE LA TERRE

Nicola van sypres
drack

Lamentabla description du nauiere a dit figueur drack eschoue et burlant co le rock le passe de 20 beures in a la fin par su grace de dieu su delivre dudict peril

avoid encountering storms or any hostile Spanish shipping which might snatch his prize away at the last moment. But his luck held, and on 26 September 1580, the *Golden Hind* dropped anchor in Plymouth harbour, after very nearly three years away on this truly epic journey.

Drake's first act was highly revealing: he hailed the crew of a fishing-boat and asked them if the queen was still alive. During the voyage home, he must have spent many anxious hours wondering about events back in Europe, about the state of Anglo-Spanish relations, and about the prospects for him personally should the queen have been succeeded by her heir, the Catholic Mary Queen of Scots. He received the answer he had prayed for however, and, having greeted his wife and the mayor of Plymouth aboard his ship, he sent a messenger to London with news of his return and of the treasure he had brought with him. The initial reply from the queen must have worried him deeply: she was displeased with him, for the Spanish were demanding retribution for his acts of piracy, news of which had reached Europe long ago, while Drake was just beginning his crossing of the Pacific. But perhaps this message was worded to satisfy the Spanish ambassador, for another private communication followed shortly assuring him of her support. He then proceeded to land his treasure which, according to one story, was stored with the help of the Mayor of Plymouth in a strong tower, guarded by forty men. Drake himself departed for London, with several horses laden with money and jewels for Queen Elizabeth. He was granted a long private audience with her, gave her an account of his voyage, illustrated apparently by a large manuscript map. Perhaps this was the same map which he acquired from Lisbon, and which people like Captain Anton and Nuno da Silva had seen, probably overdrawn with Drake's route; if so, the map now known as the Drake-Mellon map may have been a copy of it. The original Drake map was said to have hung in the Palace of Whitehall for many years, and is thought to have been destroyed in the fire which engulfed the building in 1698.

The treasure was transferred to the Tower of London, but its full extent was never finally recorded. Drake himself was allowed to keep £10,000 for himself and the same amount again to share among his crew, but it would be slightly surprising if he had not secreted something more already, during the first moments when the treasure came ashore, when nobody knew its value. The total certainly ran into hundreds of thousands of pounds, which equates to many millions in present-day terms. The backers of the voyage, including the queen herself, received back £47 for every pound invested. It is not surprising that she and her councillors steadily stone-walled the Spanish claims for restitution, especially when it became clear that King Philip was not prepared to push the matter to the edge of war; he was far too preoccupied with subduing the Dutch struggle for independence. Drake had certainly succeeded in 'annoying' Spain in the Indies, but given the vast concerns of Philip's global empire, it was still a secondary matter. Philip was compelled however to consider strengthening his colonial ports and the fleets which guarded them. Specifically, he established a fortified town on the northern shores of the Magellan Strait 'to the end that no other nation should have passage through into the South Sea'. But this settlement

Drake had certainly succeeded in 'annoying' Spain in the Indies, but given the vast concerns of Philip's global empire, it was still a secondary matter.

quickly came to grief in that harsh climate, and when Thomas Cavendish sailed through the Strait in 1587 he observed the deserted remnants of the colony.

When six months had passed, Queen Elizabeth felt it safe to acknowledge openly Drake's historic achievement – and perhaps his personal service to her. The *Golden Hind* had been brought round to London, and lay moored in Deptford where it was a huge public attraction. Here on 4 April 1581, the queen came aboard and knighted Drake, amid rather raucous scenes of public celebration. 'His name and fame became admirable in all places, the people swarming daily in the streets to behold him, vowing hatred of all that durst mislike him. Books, pictures and ballads were published in his praise, his opinion and judgement concerning marine affairs stood current,' wrote the contemporary historian John Stow later. The populace 'honoured him with admiration and praises,' wrote the historian, Camden, 'who thought it no less honourable to have enlarged the bounds of the English glory, than of their Empire.' Among the pictures mentioned by Stow was the very aristocratic-looking image by the famous miniaturist, Nicholas Hilliard, and numerous engravings, including the one by Jodocus Hondius, where Drake looks rather rounder, rougher and tougher. The first known text written to celebrate the voyage was some jingling doggerel verse by one Nicholas Breton, published in 1581, whose most quoted couplet was:

> *'Let Captains crouch and cowards leave to crake,*
> *And give the fame to little Captain Drake.'*

Before being knighted, it had been necessary for Drake to acquire land and property, and in December 1580 he had bought Buckland Abbey, some six miles north of Plymouth, from Sir Richard Grenville, for £3,400. He had also bought

Buckland Abbey some six miles north of Plymouth, the great house on which Drake spent a small part of the treasure captured during the circumnavigation. *Bildarchiv Steffens/bridgeman.co.uk*

Portrait of Elizabeth Sydenham, Drake's second wife, painted at the time of their marriage in 1585. Young, wealthy and beautiful, she was to spend relatively little time with her restless husband. *Plymouth City Museum & Art Gallery*

a house in the City of London, and had been generous with gifts and jewels, especially to the queen. Once knighted it was a natural progression for Drake to become Mayor of Plymouth and then a Member of Parliament. While Mayor, he was instrumental in bringing a modern new water supply to the town from the River Meavy and Drake had good personal reasons for doing this, for among the local properties in which he had decided to invest some of his money were a number of watermills. He sat in Parliament from 1581 until 1588 as member for the Cornish boroughs of Bossiney and Camelford. His works on various committees, including that connected with empowering Sir Walter Raleigh to set up his ill-fated colony of Roanoke, brought Drake into contact with the great and powerful in the world of politics and society. There is some anecdotal evidence, however, that he was never completely accepted by the aristocrats and grandees. William Cecil rejected the gifts he offered, and wanted as little to do with him as possible, while to others his heroic career looked like little more than piracy on a grand scale.

Another cloud hanging over his reputation was the Doughty affair. John Doughty, brother of the dead man, had remained with Drake throughout the

entire voyage, apparently carefully watched by Drake, and on the return to England he was determined to pursue Drake for murder. His moves to bring Drake to court were blocked by technicalities thrown up by Drake's friends. In his exasperation, it seems that Doughty may have become involved in Spanish plots to assassinate his enemy; certainly he was thrown into prison late in 1583, and thereafter no further trace of him can be found. It seems that Leonard Vicary and the other gentlemen sympathetic to Doughty gave up any ideas of pursuing the matter, and Drake was safe.

Drake also made a brilliant second marriage, for in January 1583 his first wife Mary had died, and exactly two years later Drake married Lady Elizabeth Sydenham. Elizabeth was young, rich, heir to the Combe Sydenham estate in Somerset, well educated and, if her portraits do not lie, she was extremely beautiful. Many observers have had the feeling that Drake's married life was slightly enigmatic as no children came of this marriage or the first, and he was never reluctant to leave home on long sea voyages. There was a local tradition that, during the long years of the circumnavigation, Mary Drake had written off her husband as dead, and was actually preparing to marry another man. That man died before the event however, leaving her a considerable legacy; then Drake returned from the grave, and was furious when he heard the tale. Hawkins and other friends persuaded Drake to forgive her, and Hawkins noted 'he did receive her back into his favour and did newly attire and array her'. There is yet another unconfirmed story that, from the ship on which Drake encountered Francisco Zarate in the Pacific, he took a slave, 'a proper negro wench', named Maria, and that she and several companions were later abandoned on a Pacific island, because she was pregnant by Drake. If this is true, it seems to mark the only, and rather sad, appearance of passion in Drake's life.

Many observers have had the feeling that Drake's married life was slightly enigmatic as no children came of this marriage or the first, and he was never reluctant to leave home on long sea voyages.

Without question, Drake's voyage was a personal triumph, yet in terms of new geographical knowledge, its results remained ambiguous, largely because of the secrecy in which the detail of the voyage was shrouded throughout the 1580s and even beyond. The discovery of greatest importance was that of the open sea south of Tierra del Fuego, and yet, because no account of this discovery was published at the time, its impact upon maps was almost non-existent. There was no map-publishing industry in England in these years, but maps published by the great cartographers of the Netherlands and Italy continued well into the seventeenth century to show the narrow Strait of Magellan separating South America from a huge uncharted southern continent. Map-maker Gerard Mercator himself complained, soon after Drake's homecoming, that he could get no clear account of the returning hero's route, nor any clues to new discoveries which Drake may have made. Mercator put forward this interesting but mistaken theory:

*The only reason for concealing the route of the voyage so carefully, or putting out different accounts of the route and the areas visited, must be that they have found wealthy regions never before visited by Europeans … The huge treasure in silver and jewels which they claim to have gained by plunder, supports this idea.'*

Even the maps which were supposedly published to celebrate Drake's achievement are contradictory. That by Nicola van Sype, issued in Amsterdam is undated, but includes a portrait of Drake and vignettes of the *Golden Hind*, yet it does not even map the Magellan Strait plainly as a strait, or give it its name. The other oddity about this map is that the text describing the *Terra Nova* where Drake was crowned by the natives, is placed in Greenland. The undated Hondius world map (probably c.1590) which shows Drake's tracks, is one of only two

Part of a world map from the
second volume of Hakluyt's *Principal
Navigations ...*, 1599. The cartouche on
the lower part describes Drake's voyage,
and this is the only world map of its time
to reflect Drake's discovery of open sea
south of Tierra del Fuego. Speculation
concerning the great southern continent
is entirely banished from this map.
*The British Library, G.6605*

maps of its time to show the Magellan Strait, Tierra del Fuego below it, and then
open sea again below that. Yet Hondius seems to have changed his mind about
this, for his later world maps revert to the accepted picture, without the open
sea. Hondius spent time in London and may have met Drake (he engraved his
portrait although he might have worked from another man's drawings) and
presumably had good sources of information, yet he shows the 'Strait of Anian',
apparently unaware that Drake had failed to find it. The second map to give
a picture of South America true to Drake's experience is the famous silver
medallion map, struck in London in 1589, and presumably issued so long after
the circumnavigation because Drake was once again in the news following the
Armada campaign. These two maps were heavily outnumbered by those which
apparently knew nothing of Drake's discovery.

One of the most interesting maps of the period appeared somewhat later,
in 1599, and happens to be the first world map to be published in England. Its
author is unknown but he may have been Edward Wright, mathematician and
navigational theorist, and the map was included in some (but not all) copies
of Hakluyt's *Principal Navigations* .... The most striking feature of this map is that
the great southern continent has been entirely banished: no land appears south
of the islands off the tip of South America. Whether this map has any direct
connection with Drake no one knows, but Drake never claimed to have
disproved the existence of the great southern continent. In the geographical
ideas which it presented, the 1599 Wright map remained unique in its time, and
the open sea south of Tierra del Fuego only entered cartographic history after
the Cape Horn route was definitively discovered by the Dutch seafarers,
Schouten and LeMaire, in 1616.

It has often been said that Drake's voyage inspired a host of imitators —

Elizabethan and Jacobean adventurers who now felt the world to be a stage, on which they could display their courage and win their fortunes as Drake had done. There undoubtedly was such a long-term psychological effect but, in the shorter term, Drake's successors found it tougher than they anticipated. The expedition that was sent as an immediate follow-up to Drake's was a disastrous failure. The plan, backed by Drake, the Earl of Leicester and some financiers from the City of London, was to send a fleet through the Strait of Magellan, across the Pacific to the southern coasts of India, and from there to plunder the Portuguese trade in the Moluccas. Four ships were fitted out in 1582, under the overall command of a soldier Edward Fenton, with Drake's young cousin, John, captaining a ship furnished by Drake. The expedition was rent by disagreement as to tactics from the first, and on arrival in Brazil they learned that the Spanish had already begun their fortification of the Strait of Magellan. Fenton refused to go further, and the fleet broke up. John Drake and his companions pressed on, but had to abandon their ship and take to the jungle. They were captured by Indians and handed over to the Spanish in Peru. John Drake, under pressure from the Inquisition, abjured his Protestantism and became a Catholic; he was allowed to live, but never saw England again. After various fruitless skirmishes, Fenton returned home with the other ships, ending one of the most ill-considered and unrewarding of Elizabethan voyages.

The expedition of Thomas Cavendish from 1586 to 1588 was planned in deliberate emulation of Drake, and in that it succeeded, recording the third circumnavigation in history. Cavendish passed the Strait of Magellan, raided Spanish ports, crossed the Pacific and brought home considerable plunder. But the voyage did not boast any geographical or political achievements, and Cavendish missed the glory of taking part in the battle against the Armada. He

died in 1591 while making
a further attempt on the
Pacific, but he has his little
share of immortality, for his
portrait and his name appear
in many maps and books of
the period, alongside those
of Magellan and Drake.

So, despite being
among the best-documented
voyages of its era, many
questions about the detail
and the significance of
Drake's circumnavigation
remain difficult to answer.
But these are the quibbles
of the historian, and the
overriding fact remains that
Drake had become the first

man in history to captain his ship in a journey around the whole world – for
Magellan had lost his life in the Philippines. The challenges and dangers, physical
and psychological, had been enormous, but Drake had overcome them all.
Perhaps its motives were not entirely noble, being mercenary above all, but its
conduct was heroic, and its repercussions in British history would be felt through
later generations. It was a feat of sustained determination and tenacious
seamanship; it commands our admiration, and it deserves its place in history.

Drake's skills and experience played
a leading role, suggesting to Queen
Elizabeth and her councillors new
tactics through which Spanish
interests might be damaged.

# 4

# Open warfare 1585–87

The third major phase of Drake's career was increasingly shaped by political events, and in England in the 1580s this meant the rising tension with Spain that would culminate at last in open war, and the Armada campaign. In this period of tension, Drake's skills and experience played a leading role, suggesting to Queen Elizabeth and her councillors new tactics through which Spanish interests might be damaged. In the early 1580s, Drake's circumnavigation and his penetration of the Spanish and Portuguese trading empires inflated English pride and led to a host of imitative plans. The north-east and north-west passages were the subject of renewed interest, while the idea gained ground that North America was a territory awaiting colonisation by the English, whether on the north-eastern or the north-western seaboard, in regions out of Spain's jurisdiction; the first move towards realising this ambition came in the spring of 1585, when Sir Richard Grenville sailed on behalf of his cousin, Sir Walter Raleigh, to establish the first English colony on Roanoke Island, South Carolina. The death in 1580 of King Sebastian of Portugal, had led to Philip II of Spain's annexation of the Portuguese crown and empire, thus making Portuguese overseas territories throughout the world still more of a target to Spain's European enemies. The first scheme in which Drake became involved after his return in 1580, was a plan to take over the Azores in the name of the Portuguese pretender, Dom Antonio, in order to establish there a strong naval base from which to menace both the Spanish treasure fleets from the Caribbean, and the Portuguese ships returning with spices and silks from the East Indies. After long months of discussion, this plan was abandoned, but it demonstrates the drift from occasional plunder towards open war which characterised these years; it demonstrates the larger possibilities opened up by Drake's policy of aggressive sea-borne raiding.

Previous page: A ship from the age of
Drake, depicted in a contemporary
sea-chart.
*The British Library, Maps C.8.b.1*

In Europe itself by 1584, the Spanish were edging
closer towards victory over the Dutch rebels, a victory which
would give Spain the power to reimpose Catholicism in the
Netherlands, and to threaten all English trade in Europe, and
perhaps England herself if she chose. Queen Elizabeth
recognised the danger, and reluctant as she was to precipitate
open war, she was anxious to block Spain's advance in any
way possible, and English men and money were committed
to support the Netherlands. In January 1584, feelings were
heightened when the Spanish ambassador in London, Bernadino
de Mendoza, was expelled for complicity in the Throckmorton
plot to instigate Catholic rebellion, and perhaps even to murder
the queen. In these circumstances, any form of guerrilla action
against Spain became almost a patriotic duty and, by the end of
the year, Drake was actively involved in preparing a major strike.
The exact route and targets are not known, but it was referred
to for a time as 'the navy of the Moluccas', suggesting that
Drake himself was to take charge of a repeat attempt on the
targets of the disastrous Fenton voyage: to pass the Straits of
Magellan, and to establish a British presence in the East Indies,
no doubt plundering whatever Spanish or Portuguese targets
could be found en route. This scheme too was revised and
simplified, partly influenced by the news that reached England
in May 1585, that a large number of English trading ships in
Iberian ports had been seized on king Philip's orders. This act
of aggression disarmed the powerful argument of the English

Map of the West Indian voyage of 1585–86, showing Drake's route through the Caribbean, and his rescue of the Virginian colonists en route home. One of a series of commemorative maps by Baptista Boazio, an Italian map-maker resident in London.
*The British Library, G.6509*

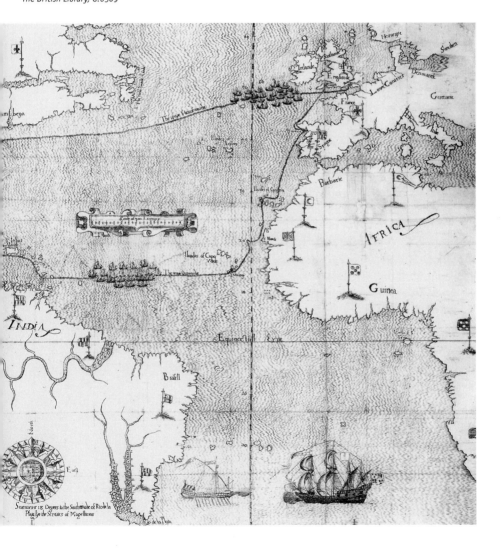

merchants, who feared that their trade would be ruined by conflict with Spain. Voices were now raised demanding that the crown issue letters of reprisal, authorising what amounted to private revenge against Spanish shipping.

In this atmosphere, Drake's embryo fleet was metamorphosed into a grand expedition of reprisal, which was finally ready to sail in September 1585, on what has become known to history as Drake's 'Great West Indian Raid'. In addition to seeking retribution for the impounded ships, the aim was to strike at Spain's source of overseas wealth – the bullion from the New World with which Philip payrolled his armies. As Thomas Fuller, the Elizabethan biographer, expressed it:

*It was resolved by the judicious in that age, that the way to humble Spanish greatness was not by pinching and pricking him in the Low Countries, which only emptied his veins of such blood as was quickly re-filled; but the way to make it a cripple for ever, was by cutting off the Spanish sinews of war, his money from the West Indies.*

More than twenty ships were assembled, plus pinnaces ready-built or stowed aboard in pieces. The list of subscribers to this venture has a familiar ring: Hawkins, Hatton, the Earl of Leicester, Drake himself, and this time the queen in person, putting in two royal ships and £10,000 in cash. Martin Frobisher, the Arctic explorer, was Drake's vice-admiral. A distinctly different point about this voyage however, was the presence of well over a thousand soldiers, under the command of Christopher Carleill, Walsingham's son-in-law, and a very experienced soldier. This expedition was plainly to be more than a seaborne raiding voyage: it was to involve invading territory on a fairly serious scale, with large numbers of trained land-fighters being used to secure the objectives. Some documents connected with the planning of this fleet survive, and they make it clear that the principal aim was to plunder or ransom half a dozen major towns

Mutual hostility had also begun to
appear among some of the captains,
especially between Drake and Francis
Knollys, a young aristocrat who carried
the nominal title of rear-admiral.

in the Caribbean and New Spain, including Santo Domingo, Cartagena, Panama
and Havana; ransom figures running into millions of ducats were predicted. The
rather fantastic idea was canvassed of leaving troops to garrison some of the
captured towns, which would then become English bases in the heart of New
Spain. And yet, once again, the expedition's status was left in the ambiguous
borderland between state sponsorship and private adventuring. Queen Elizabeth
and Drake understood each other perfectly, and she said confidently 'the
gentleman careth not if I should disavow him'. A graphic description of the
campaign was written by Walter Bigges, who failed to survive the entire voyage,
and was published in 1589 as *A Summarie and True Discourse of Sir Francis Drakes
West Indian Voyage*.

The first port of call was Vigo in northern Spain, where a number of
Spanish ships were seized, and plunder taken from the town. This was an act
of sheer bravado, designed to wound King Philip's pride, in which it succeeded.
Proceeding to the Cape Verde Islands, the town of Santiago was burned because,
after ten days of waiting and threats, no ransom was forthcoming. Yet those ten
days cost the expedition very dear, for a deadly fever was contracted, which raged
through the fleet as it sailed for the Caribbean. Almost three hundred men died
in the first wave, and a steady death toll continued for the rest of the voyage.
This was a very serious blow, and it goes far to explain the limited success of
this expedition. Mutual hostility had also begun to appear among some of the
captains, especially between Drake and Francis Knollys, a young aristocrat who
carried the nominal title of rear-admiral. This tension was to drag on without
resolution, but without coming to a crisis, as that between Drake and Doughty
had done and the animosity between the two men seems to have been personal
and social, and not related to any substantial question of policy or tactics.

CIVITAS S Dominici sita
in Hispaniola Indica Angliæ mag-
nitudine fere æquali, ipsa vrbis elegan-
tor ab Hispanis extructa, et omnibus
circumiacentis insulæ vrn dat

AA

BB

EE

DD

GG

II

Z

MM

NEC SPE NEC METV

Previous page: Boazio's map of Santo
Domingo, capital city of Hispaniola,
which Drake occupied and looted in
January 1586. The city was taken by
English land forces, seen here massing
to the west.
*The British Library, G.6509*

On arrival in the Caribbean, the first target was Santo Domingo in
Hispaniola, which was easily taken by Carleill's soldiers and then ruthlessly looted
for valuables of any kind, and the Catholic churches were particular targets for
desecration. Drake's demand for a ransom of a million ducats was absurd and
unrealisable, and he eventually accepted 25,000. Despite the violence of Drake's
invasion of his city, the governor of Santo Domingo left a remarkably generous
and perceptive character-sketch of the English leader:

*Drake is a man of medium height, fair, tending to stockiness; he is merry, but careful.*
*In command, he is forceful and is feared and obeyed by his men. He is firm in punishing.*
*Alert, restless, well-spoken, ambitious, vainglorious, but generous and liberal; not a cruel*
*man. These are the qualities I saw in him while we were negotiating.*

The next target city, Cartagena, was more difficult, not because it was especially
well defended, but because its natural position with an outer and an inner
harbour surrounded by marshy spits of land, made it more difficult to attack.
Nevertheless Carleill succeeded in landing almost a thousand men by night,
and a few hours' fighting the next morning secured the town. This time a ransom
of a little over 100,000 ducats was extorted, supplemented by the pillage of any
likely looking buildings.

By late February 1586, news of Drake's presence in the region had been
urgently conveyed to Spain, from where a rescue fleet was requested. Deaths from
fever continued to sap the strength of the English forces and one escaped Spanish
prisoner reported that 'every day they are throwing corpses overboard'. On
27 February a council of war was convened among the captains, who were
facing the unpleasant truth that their achievements were rather less than they had
hoped, and that the march across the isthmus to seize Panama was now certainly

beyond them. The decision was taken to leave Cartagena and sail for Cuba, with Havana as the last major target. In the event, however, even this aim was abandoned, and the homeward voyage was begun with just two calls made en route. The first seems to have been unplanned, the result of information gained from a Portuguese pilot, that a Spanish base existed on the Atlantic coast of Florida at San Augustin. Drake and his fleet duly located the port, landed, and comprehensively sacked the place.

It seems almost certain that the final call on the voyage had been planned from the outset, for Drake's fleet now made for the coast of Carolina, to make contact with Raleigh's Roanoke colonists. Like all these early colonies, Roanoke, under its leader Ralph Lane, was in severe difficulty, ill-prepared and lacking in survival skills. They were expecting a supply ship from England, but it had not arrived. Lane asked for a craft with which to explore the coast and Drake generously offered him a 70-ton ship and some supplies. Unluckily, a sudden and violent storm sank this ship and the disheartened Lane decided to abandon the colony and return to England with Drake. Within a few weeks of their departure, two English ships called at Roanoke only to find it deserted and the first English attempt at North American settlement in ruins.

Drake and his fleet, with his new passengers, reached Portsmouth in late July 1586, and when the accounts of the voyage were cast they made rather dismal reading. Around 750 men had died, most of them of disease, not in combat; the plunder taken from all sources failed to cover the high costs of the expedition, and the principals lost money; and the Roanoke colonists had been brought home demoralised. Yet, paradoxically, the adventure had achieved a considerable tactical success as an English fleet had roamed at will through the colonies of New Spain, had seized important towns, destroyed property, extorted

CIVITAS CARTHAGENA in Indiæ occidentalis continente sita, portu commodissimo, ad mercaturam inter Hispaniam et Peru exercendam.

CARTAGENA

ransom, disrupted trade, and humiliated the power and prestige of Spain and her great king. Among the colonists in the Caribbean itself, there was panic. 'There is no man but has suffered notable loss,' wrote the governor of Santo Domingo, 'so we have all come to extreme poverty, being in want of everything both to eat and to wear ... We have neither artillery nor powder, neither harquebuses nor men experienced in war ... Unless provided, these people are so terrorised, poor and defenceless that they will abandon the country.' From the inhabitants of Cartagena came similar news: 'In burning and looting it, the English have left this city so completely destroyed and desolate that its present condition deserves the deepest pity.'

It could be said that Drake had brought this form of guerrilla raiding to its highest development, for what had begun in 1572–73 as a private quest for vengeance had now become a policy of state, and yet still no official blame was attached to Queen Elizabeth. The damage to Spanish interests was considerable without being catastrophic, but the psychological blow was far higher, and the king of Spain was forced to take notice of the aggressive English raider whose stature as a popular hero now reached new heights. But the question cannot be avoided: had Drake and Elizabeth gone too far? The fiction of Drake's purely private status was no longer credible, and by striking in this way at the vital wealth-producing artery of Spain's maritime empire, it's possible that Drake and his royal patron had now goaded King Philip towards open war on England. Did Drake, the hero of the English defence against the Armada, actually help to provoke Spain's attempted invasion of his country? English land-forces had interfered in the Netherlands, and now her navy was threatening Spain's revenue from the Americas. Could Philip afford not to act against England?

There is no doubt that it was in the summer of 1586, when news of the West Indian raids reached Spain, that Philip began seriously to prepare his

'Enterprise of England'. His chief of staff, the Marquis de Santa Cruz, was given the task of planning the strategy and assembling the ships and men. His first plan was gigantic in scope, envisaging an invasion fleet of over 500 ships, and a fighting force of almost 100,000 men. This was soon to be scaled down, but reports of a still-massive Spanish mobilisation were carried abroad, and it was swiftly decided that England's first tactic must be to try to disrupt the invasion force long before it could reach England. Drake was the ideal man to carry the war into the enemy's camp, 'to distress the ships within the havens themselves'. A powerful fleet of royal and private, but armed, merchant ships was assembled in Plymouth in March 1587, and was ready to sail on 2 April. Drake's flagship was the *Elizabeth Bonaventure*, while his vice-admiral, William Borough, a seaman of wide experience, flew his flag on the *Golden Lion*. Their goal was to reconnoitre the Iberian ports where the Armada was being assembled, including Lisbon, and take any action necessary to cripple the enemy's preparations for war. A force of soldiers was on board for possible land operations.

On the day of sailing Drake wrote one of several reports to Walsingham, the queen's secretary, calling on God repeatedly to bless his patriotic voyage and its patron, the queen. This letter contains some words which sum up Drake's tenacious character, and which were later incorporated into a prayer, which came to be rather widely known as Drake's prayer: 'There must be a beginning of any great matter, but the continuing unto the end until it be thoroughly finished yields the true glory.' The same letter develops a note of exultation unique in the small number of documents which we have from Drake's own hand: 'The wind commands me away. Our ship is under sail. God grant we may so live in His fear as the enemy may have cause to say that God doth fight for her Majesty ...' Sceptical historians have doubted that Drake was the true author of this rhetorical outpouring, and have pointed out that he was accompanied on this voyage by Philip Nichols, the educated and scholarly chaplain, who would later write much of Drake's life-story. If Nichols did draft these reports to Walsingham, it would explain their unusual eloquence.

Only a few days out of Plymouth, while Drake or Nichols was busy polishing these compositions, Queen Elizabeth and her council were already preparing their defence should relations with Spain suddenly improve: they drafted a dispatch countermanding his plan of attack, and expressly ordering Drake 'to forbear to enter forcibly into any of the king's ports or havens, or to offer violence to any of his towns or shipping within harbouring, or to do any act of hostility upon the land.' It is uncertain whether this message was seriously intended to reach Drake, or whether it was diplomatic insurance to wave at the Spanish, but a pinnace was dispatched to carry it to Drake. However, with a week's sailing to make up, it would obviously never catch him. Lord Burghley would later write disingenuously to the Spanish representative in London:

*True it is, and I avow upon my faith, her Majesty did send a ship expressly with a message by letters, charging him [Drake] not to show any act of hostility ... which messenger by contrary winds could never come to the place where he was ... and hearing of Sir Francis Drake's actions ... her Majesty is as yet greatly offended with him.*

This diplomatic game of hide-and-seek can surely have deceived no one, for it obviously failed to explain why Drake's powerful fleet had left England in the first place, and why it contained so many royal ships lent by the queen herself. The queen had quite openly sent the Earl of Leicester to the Netherlands at the head of an English army to assist the anti-Spanish rebellion, so why should she not also send her loyal and private sea-dog to harass King Philip by sea?

A fortnight after leaving Plymouth the fleet was off Lisbon, and Drake picked up the intelligence from some Flemish vessels that Cadiz harbour was full of Spanish shipping and virtually undefended. Drake made an instant decision to open his campaign in Cadiz and set sail immediately. On informing his officers of his decision, William Borough, his vice-admiral, warned him of the danger of being trapped in the harbour by contrary winds. Drake was incensed at this opposition, but he ignored Borough in his haste for action. In the late afternoon of 19 April the English ships, led by Drake's and followed by Borough's, descended on the unsuspecting harbour of Cadiz 'with more speed and arrogance than any pirate has ever shown', as one Spanish observer wrote. The harbour and the anchorage outside were teeming with vessels laden with supplies for the Armada, but there was only one armed warship. The only determined defence came surprisingly from a large Genoese galley, which was neutral in this fight but which refused to surrender, opening fire on Drake with her canons until she was overwhelmed by the English guns and sunk. Fire from the fort onshore was ineffective and Drake now set about pounding and sinking every Spanish ship in sight. By noon on 20 April, around thirty vessels had been destroyed along with all their cargoes and it was time to leave, for Drake had no interest this time in attacking the town. At this point, however, the wind dropped completely (as Borough had warned that it might), and the English ships were becalmed until nightfall. But the setback was temporary and next morning saw a breeze carry the fleet out to sea. It had been a lightning raid, remarkable not only for its

M

Cadiz

A. The great and first fort in cadiz.
B. The second fort.
c. The Towne gate, ordnance vppon it.
d. The gallies at our comming in.
E. Caruaylcs and smal Barkes.
F. Ships, Aragozia, Biscayns, frensh, hulkes, at puental
G. Roaders at pointal.
h. a Ship of the Marques of Sta Crus.
J. Ships and gallies by port Rial.
k. gallies to haue stayd the lions passadge that way.

3 Admirals { o for the Bonauenter
             o for the Lyon
             o marchant Rial

l. the gallies dreuen back by ye Lyon

columbe de hercules.

o m. The pece that hit ye lion
o n. a pece planted for G

Isla de Cadiz

Sta. pedro.

Las puer

puental

Puer

106

Sta Katarina

Portal

el puerto de Sta maria

Rio Guadalette

a. The Bonauenter
b. The lyon
c. The marchant Rial
A. The rest of the fleete

At ther frst Ankor

d. the Bonauenter at her second Ankoring
e. The Bonauenter at her third Ankoring
f. The lion at second Ankoring
G. The rest of the fleet at Second Ankoring
h. the Edward Bonauenter a ground
J. the lion at Third Ankoring

Puerto Real

M. our fleet at Anker vppon a Brauado

W Borough

aca    20

Previous page: Map of the Cadiz raid
of 1587 drawn by William Borough.
Although the raid was a brilliant
success, Borough maintained that
Drake had acted recklessly in entering
this confined harbour with a strong
following wind, and no guarantee
of escape.
*National Archives*

daring, but also for the fortunate winds which took Drake into the harbour, and
then out again twenty-four hours later. One of the captains indeed attributed
their luck to divine aid: 'It may seem strange or rather miraculous that so great an
exploit should be performed with so small loss … but in this as in all our actions,
though dangerously attempted yet happily performed, our good God hath and
doth daily make his infinite power manifest to all papists.'

This was the raid which Francis Bacon would memorably describe forty
years later as 'singeing the King of Spain's beard'. King Philip himself is said to
have commented that 'the damage he committed was not great, but the daring
of the attempt was so'. Drake knew that, spectacular as his success had been at
Cadiz, he had struck at only one small part of the Armada. He therefore planned
to cruise off the Portuguese coast, waiting to destroy any Spanish ships he might
encounter – warships or merchantmen. He also determined to land if possible
and attack suitable towns or forts ashore, and his first announced target was to
be either the town of Lagos or the fort of Sagres near Cape St Vincent, on the
extreme south-westerly point of the Portuguese coast. Once again Borough
objected – to the plan itself and to Drake's autocratic style of command. Borough
put his case in a detailed letter, which asked pointedly what was to be gained
by the landing, then provided Borough's own scornful answer: 'No matter of
substance, neither shall any man be bettered by it, but a satisfying of your mind
that you may say Thus have I done upon the King of Spain's land'. Borough had
evidently perceived Drake's attraction for the audacious stroke which would
bring glory to his name, even if it achieved nothing else. This was too much for
Drake, who immediately had Borough arrested and confined under guard on his
own ship. So once again, as with Doughty and Knollys, bitter personal conflict
with a senior comrade seems to have been an inescapable feature of any Drake

voyage. Bold, tenacious and brilliant in his own way, Drake was unable to bear opposition to his sometimes impulsive plans.

With Borough out of the way, the landing at Lagos went ahead, but the town proved to be so well defended that the English were forced to retreat with many casualties. Sagres was an apparently formidable bastion and the fighting was fierce, but it yielded quickly. Drake himself led a party of men who set fire to the gates, a decisive move which won the battle. Basing his forces in the nearby harbour, Drake then spent several days destroying any Spanish shipping he could find, many of whose cargoes had been destined to supply the Armada. No Spanish fleet came out in any force against him. The next objective was to sail north to Lisbon, where the Marquis de Santa Cruz was based. The alarm had been thoroughly given by now, and Santa Cruz blocked the mouth of the Tagus with a small fleet of galleys. For reasons which were never explained, Drake did not attempt to attack and destroy this barricade, but returned south again. On 17 May he wrote again to Walsingham, stating his intention to patrol these waters for as long as necessary, to cripple Spanish shipping. 'As long as it shall please God to give us provisions to eat and drink, and that our ships and wind and weather will permit us, you shall surely hear of us near this Cape of St Vincent, where we do and will expect daily what her Majesty and your honours will further command.'

But almost as these words were being written, some form of fever or plague struck his fleet; Drake's plans began to change swiftly, and the subsequent events are slightly confused. The sick men were segregated, and their ships instructed to sail for home. On board the *Golden Lion*, where Borough was confined, a non-violent mutiny took place and the crew demanded that they should return to England; their captain refused, and then simply left his ship to rejoin the flagship.

One of several illustrations used to
decorate a contemporary sea-chart.
*The British Library, Maps C.8.b.1*

Borough advised the men to draw back from mutiny, but they simply turned and made for England, taking Borough with them. Drake at once convened a court martial to try Borough for desertion, and sentenced him to death in his absence. Drake then carried out a tactical shift in his fleet's operations, and determined to conclude the voyage by searching for some rich plunder. Whether he did this to forestall the criticism which he felt might await him when he returned, we do not know. He may have received some intelligence about treasure-ships in the vicinity, for he now set a course due west for the Azores. There, on 9 June, off the island of Sao Miguel, he sighted the royal Spanish ship the *San Felipe*, which was immediately surrounded and boarded. She proved to be returning from the East Indies, laden with spices, silks, velvets, china, gold and jewels – the kind of prize which Drake loved, and which 'made' his voyage, in the financial sense. On 26 June, Drake was back in Plymouth, with a treasure that was never officially tallied, but which was probably worth not less than £100,000 in contemporary terms. As before, Drake proceeded to shower Queen Elizabeth with gifts, and then divided the spoils with his co-sponsors.

In the full-scale conflict between England and Spain, which was now felt to be fast approaching, Drake was sure to play a key role.

This left the problem of Borough to be dealt with. On his arrival in England, some three weeks before Drake, Borough and the mutinous crew had been imprisoned to await justice. The trial was now convened, and this time the serious charge of mutiny and desertion replaced any personal complaints Drake may have harboured in relation to the dispute about tactics. Borough defended himself very fluently, and he justified his own actions by reminding the court of certain dark events in Drake's past. He argued that he had remained with the *Lion*, out of fear of Drake's anger and wilful injustice, which he said had claimed the life of Thomas Doughty nine years before; and as for desertion, he denied it, saying:

*Sir Francis Drake, in urging this matter so vehemently against me ... doth altogether forget how he demeaned himself towards his Master and Admiral, Mr. John Hawkins, at the port of San Juan de Ulua ... when contrary to his said Admiral's command he came away and left his said Master in great extremity ... which matter, if it had been so followed against him ... might justly have procured that to himself which now most unjustly, bloodily and maliciously by all devices whatsoever, he hath sought and still seeketh against me.*

National hero as Drake was, Borough had touched on certain vulnerable points in his character, and his eloquence was enough to convince the court and secure his release. Once again, as after the circumnavigation, Queen Elizabeth made a pretence that Drake was in disgrace, but few people believed it, not even the Spanish agents in London. In the popular mind, in the councils of state, and in the reckoning of the hostile Spanish Drake's deeds, first in the West Indies and now in Cadiz and Sagres, had raised him from the status of a private corsair to that of 'captain general of the English navy'. In the full-scale conflict between England and Spain, which was now felt to be fast approaching, Drake was sure to play a key role.

# 5

# The Armada Campaign 1587–88

It seems certain that Philip was to have sent out the Armada in the summer of 1587, but Drake's pre-emptive action delayed him in two ways. Firstly, there was damage inflicted by the Cadiz raid and secondly, Santa Cruz had belatedly assembled a fleet in June and sailed to the Azores in search of Drake. Three months were to pass before he returned, weary and empty-handed, to Lisbon, with the season now too far advanced to launch the invasion of England; thus England gained a year's grace. The exposure of the Catholic Babington plot to overthrow the queen, and the consequent execution of Mary Queen of Scots in February 1587, strengthened Philip's conviction that only the force of Spanish arms would return England to the Catholic Church. Meanwhile the Spanish master-plan had evolved and matured. Rather than ferrying close to 100,000 men from Spain to attack England, King Philip and his generals had realised the wisdom of conveying a smaller army from the Netherlands, where the Duke of Parma had established a large force. In this plan, the Armada would be needed to conduct the troops across the English Channel and to fight off the English ships at the same time. It was a simpler, stronger plan, calling for a smaller Spanish fleet than before, but its success depended crucially on the rendezvous between the Armada and the land-forces, somewhere east of Calais. When it finally sailed, the Armada would number some 130 ships – about one third of them large warships of four or five hundred tons – with some 15,000 troops on board, while a similar number were waiting in the Netherlands; the craft in the Netherlands would be purely transport ships, which would be helpless against attack from warships. The English fleet was not in fact greatly out-numbered by the Armada, and its ships were smaller, easier to handle and generally better armed. The English understood that the crucial battle must be fought at sea, for if Parma's army were to land, the chances of a successful English resistance were virtually nil.

III ◆

The Galleon of Don Pedro
taken Prisoner by Sr. Francis
Drake, and sent to Dartmouth.

Previous page: Drake's taking of
Captain Don Pedro de Valdes' ship
the *Rosario*, depicted on a set of
seventeenth-century playing cards
commemorating the Armada.
*National Maritime Museum, PU0184*

The English government was well aware that the
preparations for the Armada were being steadily moved
forward, and a defensive fleet was kept partly mobilised
throughout the winter. Drake himself wrote to the
queen 'there was never any force so strong as there is
now ready or making ready against your Majesty and
true religion.' In February 1588 there was reason to
hope for a reprieve, for Santa Cruz died. He was easily
the most experienced Spanish commander, and one
not easily replaced, but replaced he was however, by
the Duke of Medina Sidonia, and the danger loomed
again. The Duke was a distinguished soldier but, on
his own admission, no sailor, and he was said to be
privately appalled at his new command. As for the
English command structure, there was evidently a
ticklish problem here. Drake was England's naval hero,
and Spain's inveterate foe; but could this low-born
adventurer really be appointed Admiral of the Fleet,
with authority over the highest nobles in the land? The
answer was obviously no, and a clever compromise was
arranged. Lord Howard of Effingham, an experienced
sailor and the queen's chamberlain, was given overall
command as Lord High Admiral, while Drake was
designated his vice-admiral and second in command.
In the event the two men developed a strong mutual
respect, the command structure worked well, and both

Map showing the progress of the
Armada up the English Channel, and its
forced retreat northwards around the
coastline of Britain.
*The British Library, Maps C.3.bb.5*

*The Game of Bowls*, by Seymour Lucas,
1880, a famous painting of a famous
incident: Drake waves back Lord
Howard, the Admiral in the Armada
campaign. The Drake legend was fed by
narrative paintings such as this.
*National Maritime Museum, A2338*

played their personal parts in the battle. The other leading figures in the English
fleet were Sir Richard Grenville, Sir Martin Frobisher, Sir John Hawkins and
Lord Henry Seymour. Howard's flagship was the *Ark Royal*, while Drake
commanded the *Revenge*. These were both royal ships, of course, but the English
fleet was, as ever, a familiar blend of state and private vessels, as the concept of a
royal navy as a professional fighting force simply did not exist, nor was there any
distinction between the personnel in the royal ships and those in the armed
merchantmen.

In the strategic argument that went on in England, Drake's voice was raised
repeatedly in favour of an offensive stance. He argued vehemently for pre-
emptive action, which would prevent any Spanish fleet from even reaching the
Channel. He proposed to patrol the Iberian coast and seek open battle whenever
the enemy should appear. 'With fifty sail of shipping,' he wrote to the council, 'we
shall do more good upon their own coast than a great many more will do here at
home.' Against this strategy there was the awful possibility that the enemy would
not be located, and that the Spanish fleet might then arrive in the Channel to
find England's coasts defenceless. It was a difficult decision, but Drake's aggressive
policy prevailed, and on 30 May almost the entire English navy set out for
Lisbon. Within a week however they were back in Plymouth, having received
intelligence that the Armada had sailed, and they dared not risk missing it at sea.
This intelligence was correct, but incomplete: hampered by bad weather, sickness
and supply problems, the Armada had advanced no further than Corunna, where
it lay for whole month refitting. Three times the English fleet attempted to put
to sea, but each time they were beaten back by adverse winds, and they were
compelled after all to wait in the west-coast ports and prepare for battle in the
Channel.

On 12 July 1588 the Armada finally left Corunna, and was sighted off the Lizard, at the south-west tip of England, on 19 July, sailing steadily in the tight crescent formation that is so distinctively seen in the engravings of the time. News of its approach was rushed to Drake and the commanders in Plymouth, but the famous story of the game of bowls that Drake was reputedly playing at the time he received the news may be pure legend; certainly it is impossible to verify, and Drake's part in it was apparently never mentioned in any written account earlier than the eighteenth century. The English warships hastily put to sea and drew near to the great Armada. At first the Spanish were up-wind of the English (and therefore had the advantage in traditional sailing terms) but, in some unexplained way, the English quickly succeeded in manoeuvring around the Armada and gaining the 'weather-gauge', an advantage that was to prove vital as the two forces moved steadily up-Channel on the westerly wind. The Armada had no interest in engaging in a pitched naval battle with the English as its mission was to rendezvous with Parma's invasion force somewhere near Calais. The English tactics therefore must have been to snap at the heels of the compact mass of Spanish ships and, if possible, to disrupt their close formation and attack any isolated ships. For eight days this is exactly what happened and while the Armada sailed slowly eastwards, both fleets expended enormous quantities of powder and shot without inflicting significant losses on the other.

It may have been pure chance that the only contro-versial incident in these first few days involved Drake himself. Even in the midst of this vital struggle for his country's very survival, he succeeded in capturing the *Nuestra Senor del Rosario*, a rich treasure-ship which was one of the pay ships of the whole Armada. The circumstances in which he did so were complex: on 31 July the *Rosario* had been damaged by a collision with another Spanish vessel, and became detached from the Armada. During that night Drake reportedly became suspicious of some unidentified vessels sailing southward towards open sea, and he turned to follow them, fearing that they might by Spaniards seeking to mount a surprise attack from the rear. They transpired to be German merchant ships, but in pursuing them Drake had come upon the isolated *Rosario* and had demanded her surrender. The captain, Don Pedro de Valdes, complied at once and Drake had the great galleon towed triumphantly into Torbay, having first removed her treasure to the *Revenge*. This is the official story but the problem with it is that Howard had given specific orders to Drake to sail through the night in the wake of the Armada with a large stern-lantern on the *Revenge* to act as a guiding light to the whole English fleet. This lantern of course vanished with Drake's ship, and dawn found the English warships scattered far and wide, looking for their leading ship; no one else seems to have observed the German merchant

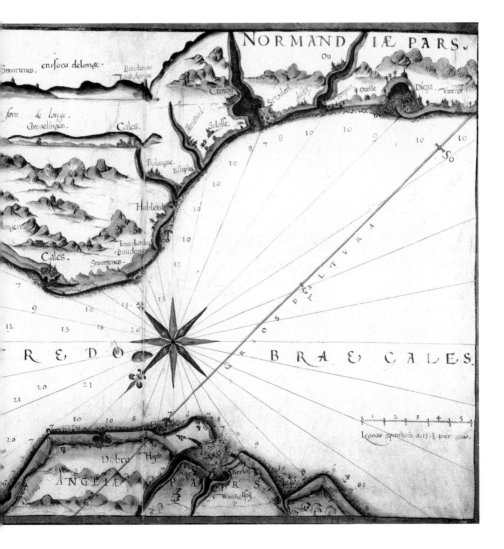

NORMAND IÆ PARS.

Swartenes. enfora delonge. Doudeman Tour deprise Ou

Croton S:t Valeri Trepor Orville Diepa Varenge
Manfroul S:losse.

foru de longe. Cales. 8 7 9 10 10 9 10 10
Gravelingen. 8 9 10 10
10
Bolougne. 10
Eslaples.
Hableru 10
lingen Cales. 10
Tourdordi 10
Doudena
Swartenes 12
7
9 14 15
12 15 18 20
R E D O BRA & CALES.
20 21
21 10 10 8
20 10 10 8

Iso

TROS DALTVRA

1 2 3 4 5
legoas Spanhoes a.17.¼ por gaw.

Debra Hyth
ANGLIÆ PA R S
Riie Rierloi Winkelseij

119

Wansteade

London

Parte of Essex

Thames

Coolyng

Grenewich

Shooters hylle

Dertford

Stone

Mylton

Cobham

Rochester

S. Marie Cray

Snodland

Byrlyng

Squeryes in Westram
Fons Flum
Da Kent

Otford

Parte of
Surrey

Juiam

Hunton

yalding

Penshurst

Parte of Sussex

Godhyrst

Hawk

Beacons in Kent.

Aug. 1585 W:L.

Crowbroe

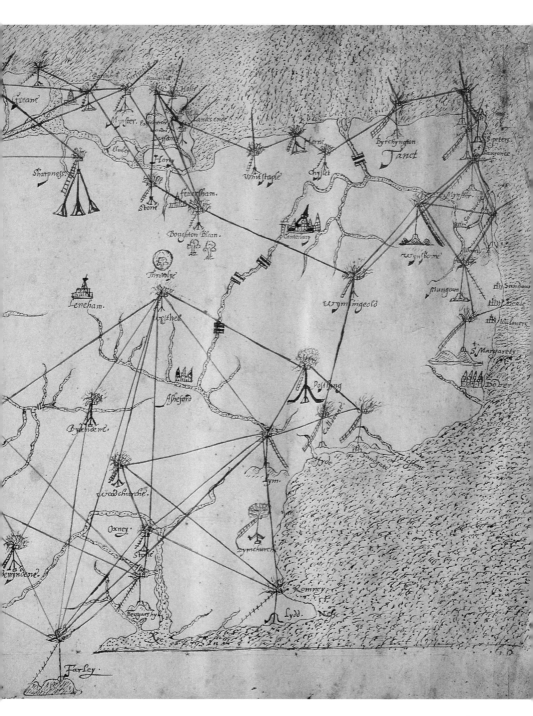

ships. (The sequel to these strange events will be discussed later.) Don Pedro's
swift surrender was equally remarkable because his ship, although damaged, was
heavily armed and contained some hundreds of fighting men. So incensed was
Medina Sidonia by this incident that he reminded the rest of his captains that
death awaited any of them who showed cowardice or deserted his fleet.

During this time, while sailing up-Channel, Medina Sidonia had been
waiting anxiously for a communication from Parma confirming their rendezvous,
but he waited in vain. On 6 August the Armada had reached Calais and at last the
message came, but, to the Spanish admiral's dismay, Parma reported that his forces
were not in place and several days would be needed before they would be ready
to embark. The Armada would either have to continue to sail eastwards and risk
being unable to return in the teeth of the prevailing westerly wind, or face the
full-scale sea-battle which they had so far avoided, and which would risk
breaking up the Armada. Medina Sidonia must at this point have known that,
having missed the crucial rendezvous with the Duke of Parma, the game was
almost certainly lost. On the night of 7 August the English sent fireships into the
anchorage off Calais, leaving the Spanish no choice but to make for open sea
with all speed – without the tight formation they had held up the Channel. This
was the opportunity the English had waited for, and it was now that their swifter

ships and more powerful guns showed their qualities. Throughout the 8 August, the Armada was pounded off the Flemish coast near Gravelines, and only a shift in the wind from west to south prevented many of the Spanish ships being driven onto the Flemish coast. For the Armada to fight its way back down-Channel would be virtual suicide, so the only course open was to sail north. It became obvious that the Spanish invasion of England would not take place and that a long and bitter voyage around the entire coast of Scotland and Ireland stood between them and their homeland. For some days the English ships pursued them as far as the Northumberland coast, before they turned around and left the weather, the North Sea and then the Atlantic to do their work repelling the Spanish ships. By this time the English fleet was desperately short of food and ammunition, and sickness had broken out among the crews. Nevertheless Drake wrote joyfully to Walsingham:

*There was never anything pleased me better than seeing the enemy flying with a southerly wind to the northward. God grant you have a good eye to the Duke of Parma, for with the grace of God, if we live, but ere it be long, so to handle the matter with the Duke of Sidonia as he shall wish himself at St Mary Port [near Cadiz] among his orange trees.*

So the remnants of the Armada struggled home, and the scarcely less weary English did the same, with Drake's position as a national sea-hero strengthened still further by a public thanksgiving and a victory parade in St Paul's Cathedral. The defeat of the Armada set the crown on Elizabeth's personal legend. The queen, wrote Camden, 'beset with divers nations, her mortal enemies, while the Pope fretted, the Spaniard threatened, all her neighbour princes, as many as were forsworn to Popery, raged round about her, she held the most stout and warlike nation of the English … not only in awe and duty, but even in peace also.'

> ... Drake's position as a national sea-hero [was] strengthened still further by a public thanksgiving and a victory parade in St Paul's Cathedral. The defeat of the Armada set the crown on Elizabeth's personal legend.

No action whatever was taken against Drake in the matter of the *Rosario*, but Frobisher complained to anyone who would listen that Drake was a cowardly money-grabber, and perhaps the incident did cast a faint shadow over the euphoria of victory. It is difficult to resist linking it with the incident at San Juan de Ulua, with the execution of Doughty, and with the conflicts with Knollys and Borough; in all of Drake's expeditions it seems, there was some episode which showed up the flaws in his character and his motivation. No one knows how much gold was taken from the *Rosario*, but it may have been comparable with that seized from the *Cacafuego* and from the *San Felipe*; no doubt Drake shared it where it could do him most good, notably with the queen. In addition, the Spanish captain, Don Pedro de Valdes, was potentially a valuable hostage, and he was lodged with Drake's cousin Richard in Esher for almost five years before his ransom was paid in 1593. Here he lived in some style, visited London, went hunting at Richmond, and apparently proved an attractive companion to Drake's elegant young wife, Elizabeth.

There has been a good deal of discussion about the significance of the Armada campaign for the history of the embryonic Royal Navy. There is no doubt that it showed the advantage of smaller, well-armed ships which could be manoeuvred in a naval battle, turning and firing at relatively long range; this contrasted with the traditional conduct of a sea-battle until that time, where ships grappled close together, with essentially hand-to-hand fighting between the soldiers on board. This was an inevitable development as the effects of improved ordnance came to be understood, and it cannot be credited to one man – to Drake or to anybody else. Likewise the division of a fleet into squadrons and the technique of sailing in line ahead, in order to deliver repeated broadsides at the enemy, has been attributed to Drake. There is no real evidence of this from the

Opposite: Report on the Armada campaign to the Privy Council signed by Drake and Howard.
*The British Library, Add. MS 33740, f.6*

action at Gravelines, or elsewhere in the campaign. Drake's presence in the English fleet was undoubtedly an inspiration – the campaign would have been unthinkable without him – but the historic importance of the Armada went beyond individuals. Spanish power had been dealt a severe check; King Philip would be unable to impose his will and his religion on northern Europe; he would be unable to secure the sea routes to the New World or the East Indies, and his enemies in England and in the Netherlands would launch new challenges to Spain's overseas monopolies, eventually securing empires of their own. Drake's was an inspirational role in the development of the English seafaring tradition, but the argument that he was a founder of the Royal Navy in any specific or formal sense is much weaker. Perhaps the truth is that Drake was essentially a loner, independent and impulsive, who functioned less well in any large-scale setting such as a fleet. Drake had played a key role in initiating the historic challenge to Spain, yet he himself would see little of the long-term consequences of the historic Armada campaign: although he could not possibly know it, Drake's greatest battle had now been fought, and the peak of his career was past.

1. Augusti 1588

Wee whose names are heerunder written have
determyned and agreede in counsaile to followe and
pursue the Spanish fleete untill we have
cleared owne owne coaste and brought the Fyrthe
weste of us. And then to whirle backe againe
as well to reinfurnall owne ship howes stand in extreme
transitie) As also to guard and defend owne owne
coaste at home without further protestatione that if
owne wante of victuallers and munitione were
supplied we woold furder pursue them to the furth
that they durste have gone.

Howard    George Cumbreland

              Edmonde Sheffeelde

Fra: Drake              Edw Hoby

        John Hawkyns

        Thomas Howard

1. August.
. . . by the coppy of . . .

# Last voyages and the Drake legend 1588–96

The Armada had been defeated but it had not been destroyed. Most of the ships that were wrecked on the coasts of Scotland and Ireland were transport and supply vessels, while fifty or more of the larger galleons had made their way back to the Iberian ports of Santander, San Sebastian and Lisbon in order that they might be refitted, re-manned and re-formed into a second invasion fleet. In the autumn of 1588, this fact was clearly recognised in England and the possibility was therefore raised of a swift counter-strike against the Spanish ships, while her forces were weakest. Unfortunately both Howard and Drake, when approached about this, were obliged to report frankly that the English fleet was itself too weakened to launch such an attack at once, and that it must be planned for the following spring. During this delay, plans for wider offensive action were developed and merged with the original idea of a punitive raid on the surviving Armada ships.

These enlarged plans were twofold – to engineer a revolt of the Portuguese people, centred in Lisbon, in order to restore the pretender, Dom Antonio, to the throne which King Philip had annexed; and to seize and occupy the Azores, as a strategic base from which to menace Spanish shipping returning from the Caribbean and Portuguese shipping from the East Indies. There were certain conceptual difficulties in this plan; firstly a number of commentators wondered why Protestant England should exert herself to replace one Catholic monarch in Portugal by another; and secondly it was not at all clear how Dom Antonio, if installed on the throne, would view English hands plundering a good part of his eastern trade. Dom Antonio had been resident in England for some years, was well known to Queen Elizabeth and to Drake and he was clearly regarded as a more friendly presence than King Philip of Spain. This comprehensive plan was plainly far more than a counter-attacking raid: it amounted to full-scale invasion

# In the name of God Amen

...Daye of August in the yere of our Lord god according to the computation of the church of England one thousand fyve hundred ninetie fyve, and in the seven and thirtith yere of the raigne of our soueraigne ladie Elizabeth by the grace of god of England ffraunce and Ireland Queene defender of the faithe &c. I ffrauncis Drake &c ... are borne to die, that the time of our departure out of this mortall life is most uncertaine, and for that we are here but Stewardes for this time to dispose of such thinges as god hath lent vs as maie be best for the glorie of his heauenlie maiestie and the welfare of our owne soules: As well in consideration whereof, as also for that I ffrauncis Drake of Buckland in the countie of Devon knighte am now called into action by her Maiestie wherein I am to hazard my life aswell in the defence of Chryst's gospell as for the good of my Prince and Countrie. And for that I haue an intent & meaninge that not onelie such debtes as I owe should be trulie paid yf god should call me before I returne out of this action and her Maiesties service now in hand. But also to giue and dispose and dispose of my frendes and servantes sondrie sommes of money, goodes and chattells and to leave behind me several thinges in a god and discreet order to remaine vncertaine or discretion that die after my decease arise or growe some issue ... of my landes tenementes leases and tenementes plate houshold stuffe iewells goodes or chattells whatsoever: whereof I am to and possessed and ... of the said ... haue inge due deliberacion considered of the premisses be being nowe in bodelie health and perfect mynd and remembrance thankes be giuen to almightie god for the same. Loe make this my testament conteyninge herein my last will in maner and forme followinge vizt: ffirst I bequeath my soule to Almightie god my onelie maker and redeemer, and my bodie to the earth to be buried and interred at the discretion of mine Executors in this my Testament hereafter to be nominated and appointed at such time as it shall please god to call me to his mercie in sure and certaine hope to rise againe to life eternall. Item I giue and bequeath to the poore people of the towne and parishe of Plymouth the somme of fortie poundes of lawfull monie of England twentie poundes thereof to be distributed to the poore people in the Almeshouse there by fyve poundes thirtene shillinges fower pence yearelie, tenne poundes thereof to be distributed to the poore people in the Maudelyn house of Plymouth aforesaide by fiftie shillinges &c ... and tenne poundes resi... to be distributed to other poore people of the said towne and parishe by the discretion of the Maiour for the time beinge and his brethren which said fortie poundes I will and ... satisfied to be paide by tenne poundes yearelie. Item I giue and bequeath to Dame Elizabeth my wife all my furniture, goodes and householde stuffe whatsoever standinge and beinge within the dores of my mansion house of Buckland (my plate onely ...epte of golde onelie exepted to be soulde towardes the paiement of my debtes) And whereas I am nowe possessed of the milles of Plymouth and by the Maiour and Comaltie of the said towne of Plymouth for terme of yeares yet enduringe and for time ... as and by the same lease more plainelie maie appeare. And of one other of ... milles named moche milles lyinge and beinge neere to Plymouth aforesaide I doe hereby graunte and devise and my meaninge and intent is towardes the better advancement of the ioynture of the saide Dame Elizabeth my wife that my Executors hereafter to be named I shall promise, devise, leate and sett ouer within one quarter of a yeare next after my decease to the said Dame Elizabeth my wife and her assignes All and singuler the milles of Plymouth aforesaid with the little closes lyinge neare and adioyninge to the same milles and the said milles called little milles together with all easiamtes profitable and advantage whatsoever vnto the same milles belonginge or apperteyninge for anie terme of ... terme of yeares to be determinable vppon the life of the said Dame Elizabeth ...

Previous page: Drake's will, which, perhaps sensing his impending end, he had drawn up before leaving on his final voyage. He did not sign it immediately, but took it with him, and made changes to it hours before he died. *National Archives*

of part of Portugal and her overseas territories. It was daring and ambitious, and Drake was obviously the man to direct the naval side of the operation, to complete the work of the Armada campaign and win fresh glory for himself and for English seafaring. In the event, the Portugal adventure of 1589 proved to be

an unrelieved disaster, which achieved nothing, cost thousands of lives, and
dragged Drake's reputation into the mire.

From the outset the expedition seems to have been plagued by problems
both strategic and practical. Queen Elizabeth's overriding aim was security from

future invasion threats, to be achieved by destroying or at least crippling the Spanish ships which lay at anchor in Santander and the other ports. But in order to achieve this, she must involve a fleet made up partly of privateers, and their interest lay in plunder. The queen provided several royal ships (including the captured *Nuestra Senora del Rosario*) and £20,000 for supplies and seaman's pay. The rest of the fleet – well over a hundred ships – were armed merchantmen, and a further £40,000 was subscribed by private investors in the City of London, at court and from the west-country ports. These investors seem to have expected that they would obtain a permanent hold on the trade arriving at Lisbon and the Azores; the military implications of a long-term occupation of this kind had surely not been thought out clearly. There was also to be a considerable Dutch contribution of men, ships and money, and this too was to prove a source of complication and trouble. That this was a major enterprise of huge national importance, politically and militarily, is shown by the involvement of the young Earl of Essex, the queen's favourite. Even before the Armada, Essex had come to know Drake, and they had discussed together the possibility of pursuing a private war against Spain. 'There is', Drake had written cryptically to him, 'some great part to be played in the Church of God by your honour and myself, if we can hold the secret.' Essex was determined to take part in the Portugal adventure and set off secretly, in defiance of the queen's wishes, to join the fleet, in search of personal glory. This incident served only to deepen the queen's anger at the campaign's miserable outcome.

Preparations went on throughout the winter, for the fleet was intended to sail on 1 February 1589. Bad weather and the slow arrival of the Dutch contingent caused more than two months' delay. As in the West Indian campaign of 1585–86, several thousand foot-soldiers were enlisted to carry out the landward

> Drake was now approaching fifty, a
> good age in Elizabethan terms, and this
> incident seems to have suddenly
> transformed him from the robust and
> invincible commander, into an old man.

attack, commanded by Sir John Norris, one of the most successful of the English soldiers involved in the fighting in the Netherlands. During these lengthy delays, the expense of feeding around 15,000 men rose inexorably, much of the cost falling on the queen herself, whose final contribution rose to a ruinous £50,000; and even then the army, when landed in Portugal, suffered from food and material shortages which fatally weakened their campaign. If a still further ill-omen was wanted, it came in the form of the illness of Drake himself. It seems that sometime during the winter of 1588–89 he had injured himself in fighting a fire in his London home and in January 1589 he wrote that he was:

*... touched with some grief before my coming out of London, with a strain I took in quenching the fire ... and notwithstanding I have and do use all possible good means by physic following the advice of Doctor French, I do yet find little ease, for that my pain, not tarrying in one place, is fallen now into my legs and maketh me very unable to stand without much grief.*

Drake was now approaching fifty, a good age in Elizabethan terms, and this incident seems to have suddenly transformed him from the robust and invincible commander, into an old man. His failure of nerve in the Portugal campaign is like the psychological counterpart to this physical misfortune.

In the second week of April, when the fleet was at last almost ready to sail, a further tactical shift in the expedition was decided. Drake had received intelligence reports that a large number of supply ships were gathering at Corunna, 'with store of munition, masts, cables and other provisions for the enemy', and he therefore proposed to make Corunna the first port of call, to deal with this new threat. What Drake did not mention in this letter to the Queen's Council, was that he was no longer targeting Santander at all, and that, after

Corunna, he intended to sail at once to attack Lisbon. When the English fleet
finally weighed anchor, it was not merely the largest that Drake had ever
commanded, but the largest naval force that had ever left England: more than
150 vessels, from pinnaces of twenty tons, to royal warships of 500 tons, such
as Drake's flagship from the Armada campaign, the *Revenge*. The Earl of Essex
had embarked with a group of gentlemen on Queen Elizabeth's own ship, the
*Swiftsure*, and eluded the message sent by the queen demanding his return. At the
final count, there were reportedly 23,000 men in the expedition, more than half
of them soldiers. It was without doubt the great Armada in reverse, an English
invasion force aimed at Spain, with only this difference, that it could not hope
to strike at the heart of King Philip's Spain, merely at its limbs.

On arriving at Corunna, the intelligence reports of a vast fleet of supply
ships waiting to be attacked proved to be false; nevertheless what ships there were
in the harbour were swiftly destroyed. But the English then proceeded to expend
valuable energy and ammunition in attempting to take the fortified town itself,
for no apparent reason. When they finally desisted and re-embarked, their
destination was not east to Santander and the Biscay ports where the Armada
ships lay, but west to Cape Finisterre, and then south to Lisbon. This was the most
inexcusable defiance of the expedition's official aims, and it ensured that they
would be harshly judged when they returned. The only tactical reason given for
this decision was the fear of the naval captains that they would be trapped by
adverse winds in the Bay of Biscay. Even before the fleet set its course for Cape
Finisterre, a number of vessels had deserted, thus weakening the force by several
thousand men, while sickness was spreading through many of the remainder.
Approaching Lisbon, Drake and Norris put their strategic plan into operation:
at Peniche, some fifty miles north of the Portuguese capital, Norris landed at the

head of some 10,000 soldiers and set out on the six-day march to their objective. The decision to land so far from Lisbon was never convincingly explained. Norris was joined by the flamboyant Earl of Essex and his personal cohort of courtier-friends and relations. Drake, meanwhile, was to sail into the mouth of the River Tagus and attack Lisbon from the seaward side.

Everything about this plan went wrong. The land-force was weakened by disease and the lack of a proper supply train. The local populace did not rise in support of Dom Antonio, hopeful successor to King Philip, who was present in person during the campaign but who clearly had little or no popular following, for 'the love born unto him is not so great as he pretendeth'. Norris laid siege to the city for just four days, before withdrawing westwards to the town of Cascaes. Essex sent a challenge to one of the Spanish commanders to meet him in single combat, a distinctly medieval touch, which the enemy ignored. But most puzzling of all was the conduct of Drake, who, arriving in the mouth of the Tagus simply hove the fleet to and waited there, unwilling to sail on and carry out his part of the plan to attack the city. Again, the reason which emerged later and which was apparently advanced by the captains in consultation with Drake, was fear of being imprisoned in Lisbon harbour by westerly winds, unable to regain the open sea. But why had this particular problem not been considered months before, around the chart-table back in England? Or even one week before, when Drake fixed his rendezvous with Norris? Such a consideration had never halted Drake before, nor had he ever been accustomed to take council with his subordinates, and bow to their advice. It is true that the sickness had taken hold in the fleet, so that, as Drake reported, 'they were not able to handle the tackle of the ships', yet they were able to sail across the Bay of Biscay, home again to England. Drake's ships lay for some ten days outside Cascaes, their captains conferring with Norris and seizing any Spanish ships which came that way, then on 8 June, they embarked and prepared to leave. There was an improvised plan for Drake to detach twenty of the strongest ships and make for the Azores, but before this could happen they were becalmed and, disadvantaged as they were, were attacked by Spanish galleys and lost several ships before being able to escape. Then after the calm, storms arose and scattered the fleet, so that even the Azores venture was abandoned and the demoralised forces arrived home piecemeal around the end of June.

Already Queen Elizabeth had heard discouraging news of the expedition and, baffled by her commanders' departure from their agreed plan, she wrote to them angrily:

*Your first and principal action should be to take and distress the King of Spain's navy and ships in port where they lay, which if ye did not, ye affirmed that ye were content to be reputed as traitors … We find that contrary thereunto, ye have left two of the chiefest places where the said King's ships lay, and passed on to Corunna, being a place of least hurt to be done to the enemy … You shall look to answer for the same at your smart, for these be weighty actions, nor matters wherein ye are to deal by cunning of devices, to seek evasions as the custom of lawyers is, neither will we be so satisfied at your hands.*

The balance sheet of this expedition was indeed catastrophic. None of its strategic goals had been achieved and the chance for a post-Armada counter-attack on Spain had been utterly squandered. An unknown number of men had died – estimates at the time varied from 4,000 to 10,000 – to no purpose. The investors had all lost money – the queen a small fortune. Many of the surviving soldiers and sailors were discharged without pay, and rioted in London and elsewhere for months. One report said that Drake was harassed in the streets of Plymouth by the widows of the voyage, although this may be only a legend. But Drake and

Title-page of *The Mariner's Mirror*, 1586.
The title-page of this English edition of
Waghenaer's great book of sea-charts
announces that it will contain an
account of 'the services done by that
worthy Knight, Sir Fra. Drake'.
*The British Library, Maps C.8.b.4*

Norris were certainly summoned in October 1589 to appear before the Privy
Council to explain their many failures. The thrust of the charges against them was
simple: first, their disregard of their instructions – to attack the port of Santander
– and second, Drake's inexplicable inertia at the gates of Lisbon. Their defence
on both points rested on their maritime judgement, that either of these actions
would have risked the fleet, and in this they both insisted that their captains had
been unanimous. Drake and Norris were not punished, but their reputations were
severely tarnished, Drake's especially, and he was not to be commissioned in the
nation's service again for six years. His fall from grace was mysteriously sudden, as
though some power of mind or body, or some guiding spirit outside himself had
deserted him. On the national level, the fiasco of the Portugal campaign serves to
correct the exaggerated claims about the maturity of the Elizabethan navy under
Drake's leadership and at the time of the Armada. The navy was still loosely
structured, still weak in its strategic planning and its command, so that any large
expeditionary fleet was at risk of the near-disintegration that overtook this one.

Bruised and temporarily exhausted, Drake spent several years ashore
attending to plans for the fortification of Plymouth, because the war with Spain
continued and Drake knew better than anyone how easily a coastal town might
be subject to lightning attacks from a seaborne enemy. He also sat in Parliament,
and naturally supported all the requests for funds and forces to resist the Spanish,
whose threat to the Protestant cause was the still undiminished shadow hanging
over all of northern Europe. Perhaps it was during these years, too, that he
collaborated with Philip Nichols in drawing up his memoirs in an effort to
restore his reputation by reminding the queen and her people of his past
achievements. The text which was later published as *Sir Francis Drake Revived* was
prefaced with an open letter from Drake to Queen Elizabeth, and it has been

THE MARINERS MIRROVR
Wherin may playnly be seen the courses, heights, distances, depths, soundings, flouds and ebs, risings of lands, rocks, sands and shoalds, with the marks for the entrings of the Harbouroughs, Havens and Ports of the greatest part of Europe: their seueral traficks and commodities: Together w.th the Rules and instrumets of Navigation.

First made & set foorth in diuers exact Sea-Charts, by that famous Nauigator Luke Wagenar of Enchuisen. And now fitted with necessarie additions for the use of Englishmen by ANTHONY ASHLEY.

Herein also may be understood the exploicts lately atchiued by the right Honorable the L. Admiral of England, with his Ma.ties Nauieand some forces forcein don by that worthy Knight S.r Fran. Drake.

suggested that this manuscript was actually presented to her, perhaps around the year 1591. In that letter, Drake reminds his imperious patron that his entire energies had been devoted to 'services against the Spaniard'.

The book may have had some effect, for by 1592 there were signs that Drake had been forgiven at court, and perhaps his health had improved, too, for he was able once again to contemplate overseas adventures and to seek backing from those who had trusted him before. His sale of his own London house for a considerable sum may have been in order to raise money for a new expedition. Discussions were long and the possibilities were many, but by early 1594 Drake had settled on an old and long-cherished objective: the taking of Panama City. Appropriately, this dream was to be achieved in a joint command with his original tutor in all things nautical and military, John Hawkins. But Hawkins's relationship with Drake had been difficult for many years, poisoned perhaps by the episode of Drake abandoning him in San Juan de Ulua, and tension between them broke out quickly on the voyage. It is not clear if the taking of Panama City was intended to hold the town permanently, for which a large army would have been needed, or raid and then destroy it. Drake, however, was on familiar territory, for it was quite certain that rich plunder awaited whoever could take Panama, and therefore financial backers could be found – ones who were prepared to overlook the Portugal disaster. In fact the readiness with which Drake and Hawkins furnished this new expedition demonstrates that the fundamentals of the privateering war with Spain had not changed: the commercial and political motivation was still there, and the maritime skills were available to implement it.

Information connected with the planning of this expedition is scant, but strangely enough a number of Spanish records have survived in the form of testimony from spies and captured sailors. In Trinidad for example, Sir Walter

> ... by early 1594 Drake had settled on an old and long-cherished objective: the taking of Panama City.

Raleigh captured the explorer, Antonio de Berrio (whose stories of his own adventures in the Orinoco were to inspire Raleigh's own search for 'El Dorado') who, on his release in July 1595, reported to King Philip what Raleigh had told him:

*They have twenty large royal galleons and another forty smaller ships ... Their orders are to go directly to the mouth of the River Chagre, without calling at any populated parts of the Indies, and put two thousand men into these boats and proceed secretly to Panama. The ships will go to Nombre de Dios, with the intention that word will be sent of their presence, and troops will be dispatched there, and the river will be left unprotected. Their aim is to take Panama, fortify it and make themselves masters of the South Sea. They then intend to take and destroy Cartagena, and winter in the Indies, destroying all the coastal towns they can.*

If Raleigh really blurted out all this information to his Spanish prisoner, he was surely very much to blame; even if the plan as outlined above is rather confused (how, for example, were the English to get their ships into the South Sea?) it still makes it clear that Drake was returning to his old hunting ground, with the seizure of Panama as his supreme goal. In the summer, however, the fleet's departure was delayed by rumours of an impending Spanish invasion of Ireland, raising the possibility that the West Indies force might have to be diverted there. In the light of this threat, Drake, Hawkins and the man appointed to command the land-forces, Sir Thomas Baskerville, were pressed by the queen and council to give assurances that they would return by May 1596 at the latest. These uncertainties and delays were swept away rather suddenly by the news that a Spanish treasure-ship had been severely damaged in a storm and was lying in Puerto Rico, with more than two million ducats on board. Although the English

from whence hee hath feathers to flye to
to the toppe of his high desires, they know=
enge that if for two or three yeeres a
blowe were giuen him there that migh<sup>t</sup>
hinder the cominge into Spaine of his
treasure, his pouertie by reason of his pe=
dayly huge payements woulde be so greate
and his men of warre most of them mer=
cenaries y assuredly would fall from
him, so woulde he haue more neede
of meanes to keepe his owne territories
then he nowe hath of superfluitie to
thruste into others rights.

This invasion was spoken of in June
1594. a longe time before it was put in
execution and it beinge partly resolued
on S<sup>r</sup> Fra: Drake was named generall
in Nouember folowinge. A man of
greate spirit and fitt to vndertake
matters, In my poore oppinion better
able to conduct forces and discreetly to
gouerne in conductinge them to places
where serbice was to be done then to
comande in the execution therof. But
assuredly his very name was a greate ter=
ror to the enemie in all those partes ha=

## Sr. Fra: Drake his voyage. 1595.

hauinge hearetofore done many thinges in those
countries to his honorable fame and profitt.
But entringe into them as the childe of ﬈
fortune it maye be his selfewilled and pe:
remptorie comand Was doubted. And that
caused her maiestie (as should seeme)
to ioyne Sr John Hawkins in equall
comission. A man oulde and Warie en=
tringe into matters wth so laden a foote
that the others meate Woulde be eaten
before his spit could come to the fire.
men of so different natures and disposi=
tions that what the one desireth the other
Would comonly oppose against. And through
theyr Warye cariages sequestred it from
meaner wittes yet was it apparantly
seene to better iudgments before our goenge
from Plymouth that whom the one lo:
ued the other smaly esteemed. Agreeinge
best (for what J could coniecture) in
giuinge out a glorious title to theyr
intended iorneye, and in not so well vic=
tualinge ﬂ̃ nabie as (J deeme) was
her maiesties pleasure it should bee, both
of them serued them to goode purpose,
for from this hauinge the distributinge
of so greate somes theyr miserable pro:

Previous page: Part of a manuscript
account by Captain Thomas Maynarde of
Drake's last voyage. Here he comments
on the contrasting and incompatible
characters of Drake and the still older
Hawkins.
*The British Library, Add. MS 5209, f.2v-3*

can scarcely have imagined that this ship would remain there defenceless
for months to come, it concentrated their minds by reminding them of the
opportunities they might be wasting, and on 28 August 1595 Drake and Hawkins
finally sailed out of Plymouth harbour. The aims of the voyage were summarised
later by Camden:

*The Queen, being advertised that a great mass of wealth was brought to Porte-Rico …*
*for the use of the Spaniard, to the end to cut off the sinews of war by intercepting the same,*
*and withal to busy him with war in another world, sent thither Sir John Hawkins and*
*Sir Francis Drake, with equal authority at sea, and Sir Thomas Baskerville, General over*
*the land-forces.*

There were six large royal warships, and twenty-one private vessels; Drake's last
flagship was the 550-ton *Defiance*. Baskerville and his second in command, Sir
Nicholas Clifford, had about 1,500 foot-soldiers under them. Drake was now
fifty-five, and Hawkins eight years older, but whether either man guessed that
this might be his last voyage we can't say for certain. Drake certainly had made
his will, and he took it on board with him, undated and unsigned, perhaps
fearing that to do so would be an ill-omen for the voyage.

Among those who sailed with Drake was Thomas Maynard, a relative
by marriage, who left a personal impression of the two ageing commanders.
Maynard saw Drake as:

*A man of great spirit and fit to undertake matters, in my poor opinion better able to conduct*
*forces … to places where service was to be done than to command in the execution thereof.*
*But assuredly his very name was a great terror to the enemy in all those parts, having*
*heretofore done many things in those countries to his honourable fame and profit. But*

Sir John Hawkins, Drake's all-important early friend and patron; a portrait published in 1620, many years after his death.
*The British Library, 491.i.6(2)*

*entering into them as the child of fortune, it may be his self-willed and peremptory command was doubted. And that caused her Majesty (as should seem) to join Sir John Hawkins in equal commission, a man old and wary, entering into matters with so leaden a foot that others' meat would be eaten before his spit could come to the fire.*

Drake and Hawkins had their first collision just days into the voyage, when Drake proposed to call at Gran Canaria to re-water, and to attack any suitable targets. Hawkins argued that this would be a totally needless delay, and Maynard noted 'now the fire which lay hid in their stomachs began to break forth, and had not the colonel pacified them, it would have grown further.' Drake got his way, and on 26 September hundreds of men in the ships' boats attempted a landing on the beaches near Las Palmas. But the English approach had been observed and the beaches were so well defended that not a single boat succeeded in landing. The attackers were beaten back, with some forty or fifty dead and nothing to show for it, and it was a demoralising opening to the new West Indian campaign. The English landed further along to coast to recover and take on water but lost more men in skirmishes, some killed and some taken prisoner. The prisoners informed the Spanish of the fleet's destination and the news was swiftly dispatched to the Caribbean. All possibility of surprise was now lost, and the call at Gran Canaria had proved to be a costly mistake. Hawkins was able to take little pleasure in Drake's blunder, for he, Hawkins, was now sick with some unnamed malady.

The flow of information to the Spanish continued after the Atlantic had been crossed, for in a storm one of the smaller English ships was separated from the fleet and was captured by the Spanish squadron which had been sent to protect the Caribbean ports. These five warships, under Don Pedro Tello, had arrived at Puerto Rico before Drake and were drawn up to defend the town of San Juan, while other ships had been deliberately sunk to obstruct the mouth of the harbour. The English fleet approached the island on 12 November, and just as they were dropping anchor outside the harbour, Hawkins died. Whatever his personal enmity towards Hawkins may have been on this voyage, Drake's mood must have darkened as he helped to consign to the sea the body of his old comrade, with whom he had sailed, fought, prospered and quarrelled for thirty years.

Drake seemed to be in no hurry to launch his attack on San Juan and Maynard wrote of the tragic results of this delay:

*Within an hour [the enemy] had planted three or four pieces of artillery upon the shore next to us, and playing upon the* Defiance, *knowing her to be the admiral, whilst our generals sat at supper with Sir Nicholas Clifford and divers others, a shot came amongst them, wherewith Sir Nicholas Browne, Captain Stafford and some standers-by were hurt … Sir Nicholas died that night … my brother Browne lived five or six days after, and died.*

Other reports say that Drake himself narrowly escaped death from this shot, having his seat struck away beneath him. That night the English launched their attack, with fireballs and other incendiary weapons hurled from small boats which they had rowed up to the Spanish frigates. Why this tactic was decided on, no one knows; one ship was fired, but the shore batteries continued to pound the

English, so that Maynard, who was in the thick of it, commented critically: 'The burnt ship gave a great light, the enemy thereby playing upon us with their ordnance and small shot as it had been fair day'. The battle was evidently very confused, and the English losses were so high that Maynard wrote despairingly 'I had cause of more grief than the Indies could yield me of joy'. By morning as many as 400 Englishmen had been killed, and Drake took his ships out to sea again. There was a council of war among the officers, in which some were convinced they could still take the town, but it was Drake himself who promised 'I will bring thee to twenty places far more wealthy and easier to be gotten'. Drake's advice was taken and the fleet drew away to the western end of Puerto Rico, where Drake paused to dispatch a letter to the governor requesting humane treatment for those Englishmen who had been taken prisoner. Drake reminded the governor that 'Whenever I have had dealings with one of your nation, I have treated them honourably and mercifully, and have set many of them free.' This letter repeatedly invokes the code of chivalry with which Drake clearly believed that he had conducted himself in all his campaigns, and it reads like a man looking back proudly on a warlike but honourable career. This expedition had been marked thus far by nothing but failure, and he must have wondered if anything could now be salvaged.

The fleet sailed south to the South American mainland where the principal target was the town of Rio de la Hacha. However, the news of Drake's presence had sped throughout the entire region and much of the town was deserted. Taking what they could find of valuables, the English burned most of the town and then proceeded west. Santa Marta told the same story: the town almost emptied, no ransom possible, the burning an empty act of revenge. Cartagena was seen to be too heavily defended and Drake passed it by, now realising that his years of aggression against the Spanish colonies had at last spurred King Philip and his ministers into fortifying them. The days when a couple of English ships could swoop down and sack an entire town in a few hours, then escape in safety, seemed to be truly over. But at Nombre de Dios the resistance was brief, and the English force was able to land and at last put into operation the core of their plan – to march to Panama. In the last days of December, Baskerville with about 700 men set out on the 35-mile overland trek, little realising the difficulty of the conditions which awaited them. The track had turned to a quagmire in the rains, their food and powder were ruined, and they were periodically attacked by Spanish snipers. Eventually, a dozen miles from Panama, they found themselves ambushed on a narrow path on the edge of a gorge which the Spaniards had blocked with fallen trees. After several hours' fighting, with ammunition running low, Baskerville realised that the position was hopeless and ordered a withdrawal. The return journey to Nombre de Dios 'brake wholly those troops I carried with me', wrote Baskerville.

A demoralised council of war followed their return, during which Drake tried to keep alive the possibility of attacking other towns, but Maynard and the others were embittered and utterly disheartened:

*We found that the glorious speeches of a hundred places that [Drake and Hawkins] knew in the Indies to make us rich, was but a bait to draw her Majesty to give them honourable employment, and us to adventure our lives for their glory.*

Sickness was now spreading through the fleet, claiming fresh lives almost daily. The fleet anchored for some days off the Nicaraguan coast, cleaning the ships and disposing of the dead. During this time, Maynard spoke openly with Drake of the sadness and failure of their expedition, and how the ports and towns of the

'We found that the glorious speeches
of a hundred places that [Drake and
Hawkins] knew in the Indies to make
us rich, was but a bait to draw her
Majesty to give them honourable
employment, and us to adventure our
lives for their glory.'

Spanish Main seemed barren of both honour and profit, compared with the great days of Drake's youth. Later when Maynard reported on Drake he remarked:

*... he [Drake] never thought any place could be so changed, as it were from a delicious and pleasant arbour, into a waste and desert wilderness, beside the variableness of the wind and weather, so stormy and blusterous as he never saw it before, but he most wondered since his coming out of England he never saw sail worthy the giving chase unto.*

This gives us a moving glimpse of an ageing hero in his last days, his power ebbing away, imagining that the world itself has changed around him, and become bleak, hostile and impervious to all his efforts. Yet, perhaps recalling the name of his flagship, Drake roused himself to a final mood of defiance in his later remark reported by Maynard:

*...in the greatness of his mind he [Drake] would in the end conclude with these words: It matters not man, for God hath many things in store for us, and I know many means to do her Majesty good service and to make us rich, for we must have gold before we see England.*

But these words were empty, and perhaps Drake knew it in his heart, for 'since our return from Panama, he never carried mirth nor joy in his face again'. At last the sickness in the fleet attacked Drake himself as they sailed towards Porto Belo, and he weakened rapidly with dysentery and other symptoms. In the night of 27 January 1596, at four in the morning, Drake called some of his men to help him put on his armour 'that he might die like a soldier'. An hour later he breathed his last. Baskerville assumed command of the fleet and made the arrangements for Drake to be buried at sea, anchored as they were close to Porto Belo. The body was placed in a leaden coffin and lowered into the sea, with trumpets sounding and all the cannons of the fleet booming across the water.

Baskerville spoke resolutely to the captains of continuing the expedition, perhaps trying their luck in Jamaica, but food and ammunition were both very low and some vessels had begun to desert the fleet after Drake's death, so there was no realistic course but to turn for home. A second squadron of ships had been sent from Spain to try to intercept Drake, and this force encountered Baskerville's ships off the coast of Cuba on 1 March. There was a fierce exchange of fire before the action broke off indecisively and the English ships resumed their homeward voyage. During this, however, the fleet's coherence disintegrated resulting in the survivors arriving by ones and twos in the harbours of southern England. The aftermath was as unpleasant as the voyage itself had been, with a huge death toll, unpaid sailors, ruined investors, the queen furious, and a nation saddened by the inglorious death of its hero.

In Spain the news of Drake's passing was received with vengeful joy, but also with a due sense of his outstanding qualities as a seaman and a warrior. Of course he was Spain's bitter enemy, but his seamanship and his magnanimity in victory were recognised as belonging to the same code of valour and honour which the Spanish themselves prized so highly. Don Pedro, who surrendered his ship during the Armada, when he knew that he had fallen into Drake's hands, declared that this was a man 'whose felicity and valour were so great that Mars the god of war, and Neptune the god of the sea, seemed to wait upon all his attempts, and whose noble and generous carriage towards the vanquished had been oft experienced by his foes.' It was a puzzle to the Spanish how an upstart, heretic nation like England could produce such a figure; as one Spanish poet wrote:

> *This realm inconstant, changeable in faith,*
> *Has raised a captain whose glittering memory*
> *Will last undimmed through future centuries.*

LA DRAGONTEA
DE LOPE DE VEGA
CARPIO.

Al Principe nueftro Señor.

& conculcabis leonem & draconem. Pfal.90.

TANDEM AQVILA
VINCIT.

En Valēcia por Pedro Patricio Mev. 1598.

Title-page of Lope de Vega's *La Dragontea*, 1598, an epic poem written to celebrate Drake's sudden death. Punning on Drake's name, the Spanish eagle triumphs over the dying Drake-dragon.
*The British Library, 910925*

Drake was to figure in a considerable number of Spanish works, historical and literary, throughout the seventeenth century, almost all them contributing to the tradition of heroism and romance that surrounded Drake's name. Even Lope de Vega's minor epic poem *La Dragontea*, written in 1598, while making great play of the association of Drake's name and character with that of a dragon, or devil, cannot avoid glorifying its subject. Perhaps the disastrous end to Drake's last campaigns, his ultimate defeat at the hands of the Spanish, made the rest of his career acceptable as a study in the ebb and flow of fortune, and in the inevitability of final Spanish victory. In England, Drake was the subject of an effusive verse biography by Charles FitzGeffrey, *Sir Francis Drake, His Honourable Life's Commendation, and his Tragical Death's Lamentation*, 1596, which ends:

> The sea no more, heaven then shall be his tomb,
> Where he a new-made star eternally
> Shall shine transparent to spectator's eye,
> But shall to us a radiant light remain.
> He who alive to them a dragon was,
> Shall be a dragon unto them again;
> For with his death his terror shall not pass,
> But still amid the air he shall remain
> A dreadful meteor in the eye of Spain;
> And as a fiery dragon shall portend
> England's success, and Spain's disastrous end.

This vision of Drake as a warlike guardian spirit of England, who will rise again in his nation's hour of need, was exactly echoed three centuries later by Henry Newbolt in his famous late Victorian poem *Drake's Drum*, with its familiar refrain 'Capten art tha' sleepin' there below?'

In retrospect, there are two outstanding facts about Drake's life and place in history: one is that his deeds clearly entered deeply and permanently into the nation's psychology, into its collective memory, and the other is that he achieved this almost exclusively through acts of theft, piracy and guerilla warfare; the problem for later historians is to somehow reconcile these two awkward facts. The key lies in the context of Drake's time. The religious enmity of the age between Protestant and Catholic nations meant that Spain was seen not merely as a political threat but as a demonic power, against whom all acts of warfare were justified. The amorphous nature of the Tudor state meant that this warfare was not rigidly planned and directed by the government, but was left to private individuals who were given to understand that they might become rich in the aggressive service of their country and of true religion; this was the privateering war, which Elizabeth's government approved and sponsored. By historical necessity, the New World of the Americas and the new sea routes to the Indies had been discovered and possessed by Catholic nations. When the Reformation threw up bitter enemies against them, it was natural that these enemies – the seafaring nations of northern Europe – would seek to penetrate the overseas trade of Spain and Portugal, and eventually build maritime empires of their own. And this overseas trade was by no means peripheral to Spanish power, as it provided the gold and silver with which her armies were sustained: to strike at the colonies and the fleets was to strike at Spain's heart. In this important historical process, Drake played a crucial role. He showed how vulnerable this

Drake, the man, remains an enigma, but his place in history is assured, even if that place has to be periodically and coldly re-examined.

enemy was in her overseas territories, inspiring others to follow where he had led. After Drake's return from the voyage of circumnavigation, the Spanish ambassador in London wrote urging King Philip to destroy all English ships found anywhere near the Americas, for 'this will be the only way to prevent the English and French from going to these parts to plunder, for at present there is hardly an Englishman who is not talking of undertaking the voyage, so encouraged are they by Drake's return.' Through his courage and seamanship, Drake achieved what others would not even contemplate, above all the penetration of the Pacific.

Historical circumstances and the wheel of fortune have played a large part in the rise and fall of Francis Drake's reputation. The concensus now is that he was a loner, at his best in the daring surprise attack with one or two ships, and that he rarely functioned effectively as part of a large force. Contemporary records about Drake's many voyages and battles are plentiful, yet even after surveying his whole life we do not feel that we know him with any real intimacy, as we do some of his contemporaries, such as Raleigh, Cecil, Sir Philip Sidney or Queen Elizabeth herself. What did Drake himself think of the circumnavigation and what did he think he had achieved? We don't know. Neither do we know what drove him always back to sea, after the Armada and after the collapse of the Portugal expedition. Why did Drake think that his last years were so cursed, so barren of the kind of heroic deeds that had marked his life hitherto? Again, we don't know. Because his inner motivation is hidden from us, he cannot be claimed as a founder of the British Empire or of the Royal Navy in any conscious or formal sense, but his inspirational role in both cannot be denied by even the most sceptical critic. Drake, the man, remains an enigma, but his place in history is assured, even if that place has to be periodically and coldly re-examined.

The 'Silver World Map', a medal
commemorating the circumnavigation,
struck in 1589 by Michael Mercator,
grandson of Gerard. It is not known why
this medal was produced so many years
after the event.
*British Museum*

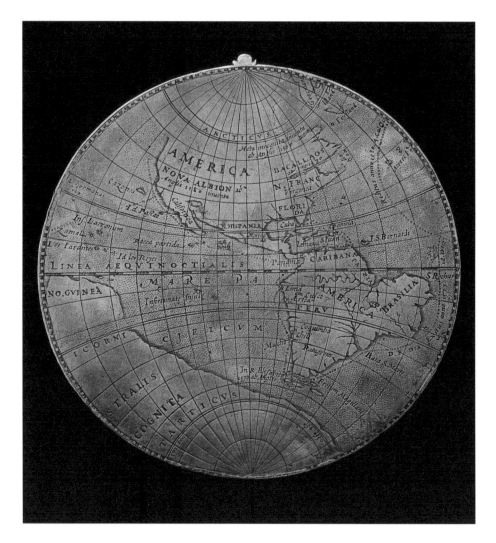

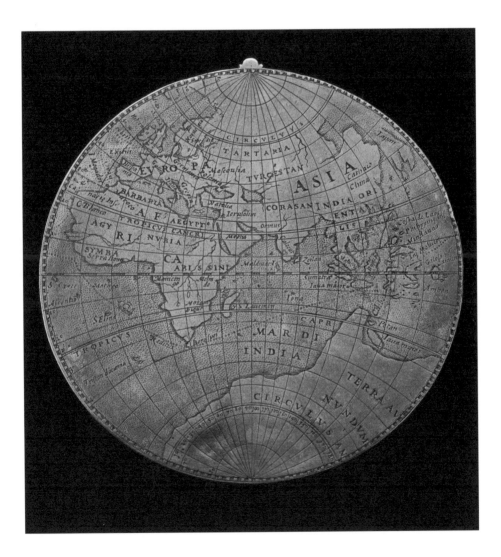

155

# Chronology

**c. 1540**  Birth of Drake (exact date unknown)

**1553–58** Reign of Mary Tudor

**1555–58** Execution of English Protestant martyrs

**1558**  Accession of Queen Elizabeth

**1562–66** First voyages to Guinea coast and Spanish Main with John Hawkins

**1567–68** In command of the *Judith*, part of Hawkins's squadron; San Juan de Ulua episode and the desertion of Hawkins

**1569**  Married in Plymouth to Mary Newman

**1570–71** Two reconnaissance voyages to the Spanish Main

**1572**  St Bartholomew's Day Massacre of Protestants in France

**1572**  Dutch revolt against Spanish rule

**1572–73** The raiding voyage to Panama; Drake returns to England a rich man

**1574–75** With the Earl of Essex in his Irish campaign

**1577–80** The Circumnavigation: sets sail December 1577; execution of Thomas Doughty July 1578; enters Pacific September 1578; rests in *Nova Albion* July 1579; in Spice Islands December 1579; passes Cape of Good Hope June 1580; anchors in Plymouth September 1580

**1580**  October, private audience with Queen Elizabeth

**1580**  December, purchases Buckland Abbey in Devon

**1581**  Knighted aboard the *Golden Hind* at Deptford

**1581**  Appointed Mayor of Plymouth

**1583**  January, death of Drake's first wife

**1584**  Member of Parliament for Bossiney, Cornwall

**1585**  Marries Elizabeth Sydenham

**1585–90** Failure of English colonies in Virginia

**1585–86** 'Great West Indies Raid'

**1587**  February, execution of Mary Queen of Scots

**1587**  April, raid on Cadiz, 'singeing the King of Spain's beard'

**1588**  June–August, the Armada campaign

**1589**  April–June, disastrous campaign in Portugal

**1590–94** Period ashore; plans fortification of Plymouth; collaborates with Nichols on his memoirs, which remain unpublished during his lifetime

**1595**  August, sails with Hawkins on final raiding voyage to Spanish Main

**1596**  January 27, death of Drake from fever off Porto Belo; sea burial

# Further reading

## Original sources

Anon., *The World Encompassed by Sir Francis Drake* (Nicholas Bourne, London, 1628)

Bigges, Walter, *Summarie and True Discourse of Sir Francis Drake's West Indian Voyage* (Richard Field, London, 1589)

Camden, William, *The True and Royal History of Elizabeth, Queen of England* (Benjamin Fisher, London, 1625)

Hakluyt, Richard, *Principall Navigations, Voiages and Discoveries of the English Nation*, Volume One (Bishop and Newberie, London, 1589)

Laughton, J.K., *State Papers Relating to the Defeat of the Spanish Armada*, 2 Vols (HMSO, London, 1894)

Nichols, Philip, *Sir Francis Drake Revived: Calling upon this Dull and Effeminate Age to follow his noble steps for Golde & Silver* (Nicholas Bourne, London, 1626)

*Sir Francis Drake Revived*, reprinted in I.A. Wright, *Documents Concerning English Voyages to the Spanish Main*, Second Series, Vol. 71 (Hakluyt Society, London, 1932)

Stow, John, *Annals or General Chronicle of England Continued by Edmond Howes* (Thomas Adams, London, 1615)

*The World Encompassed*, edited by W.S.W. Vaux, First Series, Vol.16 (Hakluyt Society, London, 1854)

## Secondary studies

Andrews, K.R., *Drake's Voyages: A Re-Assessment of their Place in England's Maritime Expansion* (Weidenfeld and Nicolson, London, 1967)

Bawlf, S., *The Secret Voyage of Sir Francis Drake* (Allen Lane, London, 2003)

Corbett, Julian, *Drake and the Tudor Navy*, 2 Vols (Longmans Greens, London, 1898)

Gerrard, Roy, *Sir Francis Drake, His Daring Deeds* (Gollancz, London, 1992)

Kelsey, H., *Sir Francis Drake: the Queen's Pirate* (Yale University Press, London, 1998)

Kraus, H.P., *Sir Francis Drake: a Pictorial Biography* (Nico Israel, Amsterdam, 1970)

Martin, C. & Parker, G., *The Spanish Armada* (Hamish Hamilton, London, 1988)

Quinn, D.B., *Sir Francis Drake as Seen by his Contemporaries* (John Carter Brown Library, Providence, 1996)

Shirley, R.W., *The Mapping of the World* (Holland Press, London, 1983)

Sugden, John, *Sir Francis Drake* (Barrie & Jenkins, London, 1996)

Thrower, N.J.W., *Sir Francis Drake and the Famous Voyage* (University of California Press, Berkeley, 1985)

Wallis, Helen, *Sir Francis Drake: an Exhibition to Commemorate Francis Drake's Voyage Around the World* (The British Library, London, 1977)

Whitfield, Peter, *New Found Lands: Maps in the History of Exploration* (The British Library, London, 1998)

Note: of these works, Corbett's was the classic Victorian biography, presenting Drake's claim to be founder of the Royal Navy, while Kelsey clearly set out to debunk the Drake legend. Bawlf is a controversial new study of the *Nova Albion* question. Sugden is balanced and readable. Gerrard's book is a delightfully racy poem written for children, beautifully illustrated, and not to be missed by any Drake fan.

# Index

Page numbers in *italics* refer to
illustrations

Americas, the, western coast *26*
Anian, Strait of 40, *41*, 42, 66–68
Anton, Captain 64
*Ark Royal* (ship) 116
Armada *2–3*, 6, 15, 88, 128, *130–31*
  the campaign 86, 90, 103–11, 112–27
  map of progress *115*

Babington Plot 112
Bacon, Francis 17, 108
Baskerville, Sir Thomas 141
Berrio, Antonio de 141
Bigges, Walter: *Summarie and True
  Discourse...* 95
Boazio, Baptista, maps of *93*, *96–97*
Borough, William 103–11
Breton, Nicholas 81
Buckland Abbey (home of Drake)
  81–82, *82*

*Cacafuego* (ship) *63*, 64, 125
Cadiz raid 105, *106–107*, 108
Camden, William 8, 9
Cape Horn 60, 86
Caribbean *22*, *93*
Carleill, Christopher 94, 98
Cartegena *100–101*
Cavendish, Thomas 81, 88–89
Cecil, William, Lord Burghley 14, *35*,
  50–51, 82, 104, 153
*Cimarrones* 28, 32
Clifford, Sir Nicholas 144–46
Cooke, John 45

Da Silva, Nuno 48–49, 57, 66
Davis, John: *Seaman's Secrets* 17
Dissolution of the monasteries 15
Dom Antonio, Portuguese pretender
  90, 128, 136
Doughty, Thomas 45, 49–56, 82–84

Dover Straits *119*
Drake, Edmund (father) 9, 12, 13
Drake, Sir Francis *1*, *7*, *33*, *134*, *160*:
  birth and youth 9–14
  first voyages 15–26
  religious motivation 15, 25, 34, 48,
    108, 135
  first battle with Spanish 23–24
  first marriage 27
  attacks Panama 28–35
  sights Pacific 32
  campaign in Ireland 37
  circumnavigation of the world 38–78
  maps and charts used by 47–48, 80
  physical descriptions 49, 98
  leadership qualities 54–56
  feud with Thomas Doughty 49–56
  in Magellan Strait 56–57
  in the Pacific 58–78
  seizes Spanish treasure-ship 64
  founds 'New Albion' 66–69, *69*,
    70–73
  wealth and knighthood 80–81
  buys Buckland Abbey 81
  portraits of 81
  mayor of Plymouth and M.P. 82
  second marriage 83–84
  geographical discoveries of 85–86
  West Indian raid 92–99
  coat of arms *103*
  Cadiz raid 104
  role in Armada 116–26
  Gravelines report *126*
  Armada report *127*
  Portuguese campaign 128–38
  will *129*, 144
  physical decline 133
  plans taking of Panama 140
  illness and death 149
  legend and fame 150–53
  historical significance 17, 25, 90,
    102, 125–26, 152–53
Drake, John (brother) 29, 32

Drake, John (cousin) 45, 88
Drake, Joseph (brother) 29
Drake, Thomas (brother) 45
Drake's Bay (California) 72
'Drake's Drum' (poem by Newbolt) 152
Drake-Mellon map *46–47*, 48

'Elizabeth Islands' (South America)
  58, 61, *61*
Elizabeth, Queen *18*, 21, 38, 79–81,
  *83*, 92, 104, 122, *123*, 124, 132–37
Enriquez, Martin 23–24
Essex, Earl of 37, 51, 132, 136

Fenton, Edward 88
FitzGeffrey, Charles 151
Fletcher, Francis 45, 77
Foxe, John: *Book of Martyrs*, 15, 48
Frobisher, Martin 94, 116, 125
Fuller, Thomas 94

Game of Bowls, legend and painting
  116–17, *117*
*Golden Hind* (ship, formerly *Pelican*)
  44, *44*, 56, 57, 77, *77*, 81
Gonson, Benjamin 20
Gravelines, Battle of 124
Grenville, Sir Richard 43, 81, 90, 116

Hakluyt, Richard: *Principal
  Navigations...* 16, 67, 86, *87*
Hatton, Sir Christopher 46, 51, 57
Hawkins, Sir John 14, 17–27, 111, 116,
  140–45, *145*, 146
Henry VIII and the English navy
  15–16
Hilliard, Nicholas 8, 81, *130–31*
Hondius map of circumnavigation
  *52–53*, 54, 86
Howard of Effingham, Lord 114
Howes, Edmund 6

*Jesus of Lubeck* (ship) *19*, 21–26
*Judith* (ship) 22, 24

Kent and East Sussex map *119*
Knollys, Francis 95

*La Dragontea* by Lope de Vega 151, *151*
Lane, Ralph 99
Le Testu, Guillaume 33–35
Lovell, John 21
Loyasa, Garcia 57

Magellan Strait 38, *55*, 56–58, *58–59*,
 60, 89, *89*
Maria (slave-girl) 84
*Marigold* (ship) 59–60
*Mariner's Mirror, The 139*
Maritime politics in Elizabethan age
 14–17, 38, 40, 126, 128, 152–53
Mary Queen of Scots 79, 112
Mary, Queen, persecution of
 Protestants 12, 15
Maynard, Captain Thomas 142–49
 account of Drake's last voyage *143*
Medina-Sidonia, Duke of 114, 122, 124
Mendoza, Bernardino de 92
Mercator, Gerard 47, 85
Millway, Anna (Drake's mother) 13
*Minion* (ship) 21–24

Newman, Mary (Drake's first wife) 27,
 56, 84
Nichols, Philip 27, 104, 138
Norris, Sir John 37, 133–38
*Nova Albion* ('New Albion') 66, *67*,
 68–73

Oxenham, John 32–33, 43–44, 62

Panama, strategic importance of
 28–29, 140
Parma, Duke of 112, 122, 124
*Pasco* (ship) 29
Phillip II, King of Spain 14, *14*, 80, 90,
 102–103, 112, 126
Pike, Robert 33
Plate of brass *70–71, 72*
Plymouth 10–11
 and West Country sea trade 17

Raleigh, Sir Walter 82, 90, 140–41,
 153
*Revenge* (ship) 116, 135
Roanoake Colony 99
*Rosario* (ship) *113*, 118, 125

San Juan de Ulua, battle of 23–25
Santa Cruz, Marquis de 103, 109, 114
'Silver medallion map' of
 circumnavigation 86, *154–55*
*Sir Francis Drake Revived* 30, *30*, 31,
 38, 138
Spice Islands *74–75*, 76–77
St Bartholomew's Day Massacre 34
Stow, John 8
*Swan* (ship) 29
Sydenham, Elizabeth (Drake's second
 wife) 83–84, 125

Tello, Don Pedro de 146
Thorne, Robert 40
Throckmorton Plot 92
Tilbury address *123*
 route map *122*

Valdes, Don Pedro de 118, 125
Van Sype map of circumnavigation
 *78–79*, 85
Vicary, Leonard 46, 51

Walsingham, Sir Francis *34*, 41, 51,
 124
*World Encompassed, The* 8, 45, *45*, 61,
 67
Wright, Edward 86
Wynter, John 44, 59–60
Wynter, William 20

Zarate, Francisco de 65